The Codependency Recovery Guide

How To Overcome Fear of Abandonment, End People Pleasing and Conquer Codependent Behavior

By

Damian Blair

Disclaimer

Table of Contents

Introduction

Do you feel like other people are running your life? Do you feel like you are living solely for others and neglecting yourself?

If so, you are not alone.

According to a study by Kent State University, codependency affects nearly 40 million Americans and is one of the leading causes of depression in North America. Codependency can leave you feeling unloved, ignored, and unappreciated. You might find yourself having a hard time making decisions for yourself or find that others are manipulating you. You may even have a hard time identifying this pain as valid because you are so used to these feelings being part of your life.

You might find yourself wondering "Is something wrong with me?"

You picked up this book because you are feeling like you have lost sight of yourself. Likewise, you might be questioning the health of your relationships or feel overburdened by one. You might be feeling guilt or shame for taking care of others in a toxic or dysfunctional cycle-- but you keep doing it.

The codependent loop relies on the fear that you are failing someone. Fear that you are not good enough. Fear that you won't be able either to abandon the person or to do your best in your relationship. You base your decision on this fear instead of choosing what you know is right, rooted in honesty and trust of oneself. It's a self-perpetuating problem.

But there is a way out.

The Codependency Recovery Guide was written to teach you how to break the cycle of codependency and put you on the path towards healing and growth.

Who Wrote This Book?

My name is Damian Blair. As a retired couple's therapist, I have witnessed the damaging effects of both codependent and narcissistic behavior throughout the lives of my clients. I wrote this book to help those who find themselves unable to break free from cycles of codependent behavior. This book was written to allow you to find your true voice and not be taken advantage of by others. My hope is that after reading this guide you will have the knowledge you need to move forward towards recovery.

What You Will Learn

In the first chapter, you will learn how to recognize traits of codependency. You will learn how it originates and what the key indicators are. You will also learn the differences between dependent and codependent behaviors.

In the second chapter, we will examine the relationship between codependency and narcissism. You will discover how to avoid and overcome the narcissistic cycle. You will learn the intricacies of being a codependent empath and how to end a dysfunctional relationship with a narcissist.

In chapter 3, you will learn how to let go and break the pattern of being an enabler to others. Enabling behaviors includes giving money, lying, making excuses for others bad behavior, or helping with an addiction. This section is dedicated to breaking the pattern.

Chapter 4 is all about communication styles. You will learn how to overcome negative communication patterns and be more assertive. We will examine the external behaviors and change the way others perceive you.

In Chapter 5, we will discuss how to set boundaries. You will learn how to compassionately say no (and mean it) as well as how to be assertive without being aggressive. You will also learn how to set limits on the people in your life who are using you as an enabler.

Chapter 6 will teach you how to detach. This process of detachment will allow you to stop giving your power away and start taking it back. You will learn how to break away effectively and lovingly, without guilt or shame.

In Chapter 7, you will learn how to stop being a people pleaser. You will discover practical steps to get out from under the control of others, while acknowledging and correcting negative patterns of being everyone's go-to source.

Chapter 8 will show you how to begin the process of rediscovering yourself. You will learn self-awareness exercises and how to develop a clear focus for your life. You will start to listen to the voice within.

And finally, in Chapter 9, you will be given practical self-assessment exercises that will put you on the path towards recovery and develop your skills of greater self-awareness.

The Codependent Recovery Guide isn't a book on how to avoid toxic people, but a practical guide on breaking the negative patterns that keep you trapped in toxic cycles of codependency.

Ready to get started? Turn the page and let's take the first step together!

Chapter 1. Recognizing Codependency

Do you hate disappointing other people? Do you often feel obliged to do something that's not beneficial to you, just so that other person won't be upset? Do you give a lot, but rarely get anything in return? If you can relate to any of these situations, you might be codependent.

Codependency is also established when you are emotionally or psychologically reliant on a partner to an excessive degree. This might happen when your partner needs you to provide them with emotional support due to mental illness or because they have an addiction.

Someone who is codependent needs to feel needed, even if they are angry and upset when other people use their help or take advantage of them. A person who is codependent is usually portrayed as caring and as someone who will put other people's needs before their own.

However, this isn't always true.

People who put others before themselves can be angry and spiteful, even acting outwardly vengeful. It's not always nice behavior. People who are codependent are not always performing the good deeds solely because it is the right thing to do. Their motives may be totally unrelated to the person in need of their assistance.

The primary reason codependent people behave the way they do is because they are scared of confrontation. They struggle to navigate relationships and find it difficult to say no. They are scared of upsetting their significant other, friend or loved one-- so they do what they are told, even when it means making big personal sacrifices.

Codependents are usually people who lack self-confidence and get fulfillment by being there for others. They often do things to help another person's problems, even if it's something that goes against their best interests. Codependent relationships are unhealthy because they are based on maintaining a dysfunctional status quo. The codependent partner believes that their happiness comes from controlling the other person, and the dependent partner feels cared for.

Ultimately, relationships based on codependency suppress the independent self where the codependent person is not able to do anything for themselves.

Where Does It Start?

Codependency is a psychological and behavioral condition that's often rooted in childhood. Many cases of this condition come about because of parents with poor boundaries. This condition usually begins with a need to be needed. It develops when we are children and continues into adulthood. The cycle perpetuates in order to feel loved, valued, or worthy of affection.

If grow up believing your own needs don't matter, you learn to ignore what you think, feel, and want. Consequently, you are unable to assert yourself and ask for things when these needs are not met. You may have had to take care of an aging primary caregiver, or someone with health problems, which pushed you in a new direction. The caretaking behaviors you learned might have felt like they were natural and transferred over into future relationships. You might've grown up trying to make as many people happy so you could hold onto them and their affection.

The following are some common scenarios that usually lead to codependency in adult life:

- Physical or emotional abuse.
- Parents or caregivers that always put themselves before the needs of their children.
- A caregiver with a personality disorder, which may inhibit you from expressing your own feelings.
- Criticism and insults from parents, siblings, or peers that leave you feeling insecure in relationships.

- The loss of one or both parents, leading to you fearing future abandonment.
- A controlling parent or caregiver who doesn't let the child learn and set their own limits.

Is It A Mental Illness?

The Diagnostic and Statistical Manual of Mental Disorders, 5th Edition, from the American Psychiatric Association, is a classification system for mental health disorders. Mental health experts have advocated for codependency to be recognized as an officially diagnosable illness since 1986. However, at the time of this publication, the DSM-5 has not officially recognized codependency as a mental disorder.

Codependency is characterized by a person who has lost their identity and seeks to gain it through someone else. It's not a mental illness. However, in some cases codependency can be a precursor to developing a mental illness

The Key Indicators of A Codependent Relationship

Even though codependency is not a recognized mental illness, many people have an addiction to control others or be controlled by them. The first step in dealing with a codependent relationship is to identify if you have one. Codependent relationships are typically characterized by an over-reliance on the other person for various needs as well as a constant desire to control and fix things. Living with somebody else who also feels just as needy as you does not give either of you the chance to be independent. You share the same level of anxiety.

When people make themselves seem like a doormat, then that is the role they play in any relationship. Breaking that expectation is difficult without improving your self-care habits. If you let someone else yell at you when you make a mistake, it will inevitably happen again.

Common Codependent Traits

Codependents have an uncanny ability to let the needs of everyone and anyone around them come before their own. They often avoid difficult conversations when they are not in a position of control and neglect to represent their own needs as important. With an increased awareness of codependents in society, it is critical to look closer at one's self and understand whether one has a tendency to become overly dependent on others. Since codependency is not a mental health diagnosis, it has its own distinct types of characteristics and behaviors. These can be identified as Cognitive, Emotional and Behavioral.

Cognitive Traits

1. You have difficulty identifying thoughts as your own.

Being codependent can have a deep impact on an individual because it causes them to detach from their own thoughts. When that happens, all they are left with is their external view of the world through someone else's perspective.

Your thoughts are yours before anyone else has a chance to influence them, but it can sometimes be difficult to determine where they belong. It isn't just the problem of whether or not you're listening to someone else, but if it's you talking.

2. You have trouble communicating your needs.

Do you feel like you are not able to ask for the things you want or need, or do you feel guilty when you speak up? Do you worry about your partner's opinion of your own needs? One of the traits of codependency is feeling like your own needs are unimportant. You might be so afraid of being rejected that you are unable to open up, which inevitably leads to terrible communication and misunderstandings.

3. You adopt other people's desires as your own.

Another common cognitive trait of codependency is to adopt other people's ideas as your own. When this happens, you may find it difficult at first to recognize that you're not taking responsibility for your own thoughts and actions. Codependency disrupts the thinking function of the natural self. It forces you into a pattern of making decisions based on how they impact someone else rather than what is best for you.

Emotional Traits

1.   You are unable to deny other people's requests.

If you find that you can't deny someone's requests, then you might have a problem. You are feeling guilty if you tell them 'no' and can't sleep at night because of this fear of rejection. It might seem like a good idea to say 'yes' quickly in order to avoid upsetting the other person, but after a while you might notice that you go through life avoiding an affirmative 'no'.

2.   You have a paralyzing fear of not being loved or accepted.

Do you fear that you won't be loved or accepted if you don't sacrifice all your needs to those of others? Codependent people often feel guilty for having their own needs, desires and preferences. You might believe that if you don't sacrifice all your needs to those of the other person, you will be abandoned or rejected and left all alone.

3.   You have feelings of low self-esteem.

We all want to be loved and cared about, but what happens when you find yourself acting against your own best interest because it's the way a partner would want you to behave? There are various signs and symptoms of low self-esteem. One very common one is the inclination to make others happy at the expense to your own happiness. Some other examples are lack of confidence in yourself, including a refusal to take opportunities for fear that it might upset someone else.

Behavioral Traits

1.   To avoid being lonely, you engage in relationships that might harm you.

One of the most noticeable things about codependency is that the person suffering from it fears being alone. This is because they never feel good about themselves unless they are 'accepted or loved by someone else'. A harmful relationship for a codependent is problematic. You and your partner might feel like you are grasping at straws to keep the other person with you. The downside to this is feeling needy and relying on the other person for your personal satisfaction.

2. You take on more responsibilities than you can handle.

There are many things that can determine our need to take on more responsibilities than we can handle. People-pleasing, guilt, low self-esteem, and being approval seekers are but a few of the traits that are part of codependence.

3. You get swept up in other people's problems.

You might be codependent if all of your relationships are centered around rescuing people, or if you feel like your value is defined by being needed or helpful. You might be one to analyze the situation, assign blame or even hand out advice. You put your energy into this person's life to the point that their problems feel like they are yours.

4. You try to solve people's problems when they don't ask for help.

Just like the previous trait, codependents take on other people's problems without them asking for help. They are unable to see from the other person's point of view and are driven by a fear of abandonment.

5. You are unable to set boundaries with what you share with others.

You struggle setting boundaries because you aren't sure if those limits are going to be respected by the other party in the situation. In codependent relationships, one partner struggles with setting and maintaining boundaries because they place an unhealthy amount of emotional importance on the needs of the other person.

Codependency ultimately makes it difficult to maintain healthy boundaries, prevent emotional harm and to make decisions on your own. With these characteristics, emotionally abusive partners or friends might sometimes seem like the only option. You may feel a loss of purpose if unable to help others. Consequently, it will be difficult to focus on your own needs if you devote yourself to every person around you. Here are some situations where a lack of healthy boundaries might cause conflict:

- Despite your need for a few days to yourself, you help your friend move during the weekend.
- You agree to help a colleague, even though it means leaving your own work unfinished.
- You always step in when your sister has an argument with her husband.
- A coworker asks you to lie for them to cover up their mistakes.
- Giving financial support to someone who cannot retain work due to sobriety issues.

Ultimately, a lack of healthy boundaries can make it hard to know when you're helping or hurting someone else. There are many love languages, but codependency isn't one of them.

The Roles of a Codependent

With a lack of boundaries, codependents take on different roles to serve other individuals. They do so to secure feeling-bound relationships that guarantees their own sense of worth and significance in society. Let's take a deep look at the 5 main types: the Caretaker, Controller, Denier, Represser and Enabler.

The Caretaker

The caretaker role goes without question as the most common behavior of a codependent. This means that they are concerned about the needs and well being of those around them often at the expense of their own needs. In a codependent relationship, the caretaker is always asking what needs to be done. They want to "fix" the other person and take on responsibility for their feelings.

It's important to understand that a codependent person is not the one who encounters an issue or addiction, but rather the person they rely on for support. The individual who is afflicted with the addiction or illness needs to be cared for much like a child.

The Controller

Codependent partners in a relationship usually have a higher tendency to control the other. They want to make sure that the person they are with gets their way in everything and surrendering is not an option.

If you find yourself constantly worried about the decisions that your partner is making, then you are exhibiting controlling behavior.

The Denier

Another common trait of a codependent is denying their own feelings. People become codependents because they find themselves always trying to protect someone else, usually someone very close to them. This frequently appears when one person takes responsibility for another person's emotions and actions. People often live with the false belief that their feelings are worth less than the feelings of others. After all, the logic goes, if you're not willing to aggressively defend your own emotions, then how can you expect others to show loyalty to you?

Denying your own feelings makes it difficult for the other person in your life to realize how you are feeling. The lack of a response could be interpreted as them not being good enough, or that you're devoid of expression.

The Represser

Codependents tend to repress their anger, which leads to resentment. Often they will have negative thoughts about themselves and others, even going as far as blaming themselves for things that are not their fault. Codependents typically keep their anger and resentment bottled up until it finally explodes trigging stress, anxiety, physical illness, and emotional problems.

Codependents do not allow themselves to feel their anger. However, they can become resentful of other people and their accomplishments. This blocked anger, if it is not addressed, can lead to passive-aggressive behaviors.

The Enabler

A codependent person is often defined as a supportive individual to their friends, family or colleagues — but too much help can turn into enabling. An often-misunderstood aspect of codependency is enabling other people's bad habits. Codependent people don't like to say 'no'; they'll do anything for someone else, and this includes ignoring their faults.

They enable other people's negative traits, refuse to speak up against any harmful action, and push themselves out of the equation for the sake of making the other person happy. However, the person for whom they act as a support network is just as reliant on their illness or their addiction to give them meaning.

When Codependency Becomes Pathological

Codependency usually begins innocently by unselfishly caring for others. Chronic codependency always becomes pathological over time as it's no longer about concern for others, but more about being concerned with one's own needs being met. As previously discussed, codependency is not an illness, but a behavior pattern. Symptoms of pathological codependency involve obsessive worrying, clinging to the needy person in times of crisis, controlling too much and neglecting one's own needs or desires.

Pathological codependency is diagnosed when it becomes an addiction or negatively influences other parts of the person's life. Obsessive love can lead to obsessive thoughts and unhealthy dependence on another person, where one might neglect work or school because they want to fulfill another's desires or their request for help.

Codependency vs. Dependency

To a certain degree, dependency within relationships is healthy. There will inevitably be times when you don't have anyone else to rely on, and most people need the companionship and support that comes from other people. Every relationship benefits from helpful, willing partners—this is known as an interdependent relationship. In a broad sense, you are not drawing value from helping the other person through self-sacrifice, but are available to support them when they need it.

Codependency is often confused with dependency. In its truest form, dependency means that you rely on someone for certain things because they have the necessary experience in a given area. Codependency, however, is when a person needs to either mentally or physically rely on someone else in order to function properly. Average dependency is the same, except a codependent person's long-term goals are, more often than not, tied to their partner and their acceptance.

The Stages of Codependency And Their Recovery Process

True recovery from codependency is about allowing yourself to become a full-functioning individual, with an identity that is shaped by your own inner thoughts and feelings, rather than what others want or expect from you. The ultimate goal of codependency recovery is to be the best version of oneself. This includes trusting oneself, valuing oneself, and being able to live life successfully.

It is important to identify the stages of codependency because it is a gradual process that happens over a significant amount of time, such as months or years and may not be noticeable until it is too late. The longer codependency is left undetected and untreated, the more complex it become. The following stages are outlined in the context of a romantic relationship, but can also apply to codependent relationships with friends or family.

Beginning Stage

The beginning stage of codependency is when you become overly attached to another person and, in some cases, display actions that are harmful to yourself and the relationship. This stage of a romantic relationship might revolve around increased attention, dependency and the desire to please your partner. You can develop unhealthy attachments in a relationship when you obsess over someone, deny their flaws, doubt their feelings, give up on friends and hobbies, and neglect yourself.

During the beginning stages of recovery, you will begin to reclaim your sense of self. You start to come to terms with the reality of the situation, and embrace change. Your life starts to change once you start to see the relationship for what it really is. This is usually prompted by a triggering event or moment that serves as a catalyst for seeking help. This starts by getting more information and reaching out for support.

Intermediate Stage

During this intermediate stage, there is some increased effort to try to minimize the painful aspects of a relationship, but guilt and anxiety start to set in. The relationship becomes more overwhelming, and you sacrifice more of yourself to maintain it. You grow increasingly angry, disappointed, and resentful. Meanwhile, you change your partner by manipulating them or withdrawing from friends and family. You may also try to avoid conflict and hide problems. Your mood gets worse, and you'll become more obsessed, dependent, or more compliant.

The intermediate stage of recovery is when you are able to make new friends and get involved in outside activities. You are also able to assert yourself and maintain healthy boundaries. Through practicing nonattachment, self-responsibility begins to grow. With increased self-awareness and self-examination, your addiction will begin to diminish.

Final Stage

In the final stage, emotional and behavioral symptoms can affect your physical health. You may suffer from stress-related disorders, obsessive-compulsive behavior, or addiction. Your self-esteem also decreases. You feel hopeless, angry, and depressed. Worse yet, you stop caring for yourself.

In the final stage of recovery, happiness and self-esteem is internalized. You no longer depend on others. Instead, you gain knowledge of yourself and become independent, while still being able to enjoy deep relationships with other people.

During the process of healing, the changes in behavior and thinking become progressively more internalized. As a result, the skills and methods used as treatment are transformed into healthy habits. You feel an amplified sense of energy, with an increased ability to formulate and follow your own plans.

In this section, we learned how to identify codependency in all its forms and how to identify your own type of codependency. In the next chapter, we will discuss how narcissism adds a dangerous layer to the toxic cycle of codependency and how it can be overcome.

Chapter 2. Codependency And Narcissism: A Dangerous Trap

In many self-help journals, codependency and narcissism are often portrayed as polar opposites. Codependency is often associated with being too selfless, while narcissism is linked to being extremely selfish. Many narratives characterize codependents as victims of narcissists. Oversimplifying this statement neglects the truth that, in both codependency and narcissism, lack of a healthy sense of self can be a driving force behind their behavior.

Narcissism and codependency are both related to an insecure self. Theses types of people often try to establish or regain a sense of who they really are. People with these conditions often find it difficult to define themselves on their own. This can mean that they place a lot of importance on what others think of them. Individuals with Narcissistic Personality Disorder (NPD) focus intensely on themselves, refusing to understand others' feelings and needs. Narcissists think of the feelings of others in relation to their own selves. They are less likely to have a high sense of self-worth without others boosting it for them. They need to be surrounded by people who give them attention and admiration to feel good about themselves.

On the other hand, people with codependency often put others before themselves. They may base their identity around serving someone else. Unlike the praise-seeking narcissist, codependents crave gratitude, and a sense of being valuable. From outside appearances, narcissism and codependency may seem to do the trick at making one feel loved or important. However, in both cases this comes at the cost of relying on others' approval exclusively.

People who are codependent often share experiences with those who have NPD, but they may have adapted differently. For example, two siblings from the same household may have grown up thinking they are only worthwhile if they are useful to someone else. One of the siblings develops a high self-esteem as a defense mechanism, while the other does not and becomes more codependent in nature. Even though these codependent and narcissistic siblings have different personalities, they both share a broken sense of self and distress at the core.

Codependents need the narcissist in order to feel alive and bring themselves up. It is also a case of opposites attract, but in an unhealthy way. Narcissists will make a codependent person feel loved, needed, confident, and retain a sense of purpose... but at the same time take advantage of them. Narcissists lack empathy and may cling tightly to the one they love or need for validation. They marry codependents because they need to feel this sense of being loved. Suddenly, the partner that feels nothing returns massive attention, their self-esteem improves, and they feel important for the first time.

One troubling question for the codependent is why they might be with a narcissist. Is there something about their past or current situation that makes them vulnerable to being with a narcissist? Or are they simply attracted to narcissistic-type traits?

Codependents are typically attracted to narcissists because their lack of empathy and complete focus on themselves validates a codependent's self-worth. Through the narcissist, codependents find an unconscious echo of their pain and victimhood and this makes it all the more bearable for them.

The narcissist and the codependent have complementary roles, each one filling the other's needs. The codependent person is a partner who is able to give 100% to their loved one, and the narcissistic person has found someone who will attend to them. This can be exhausting and unhealthy for codependent people, who sometimes try to keep up with their partner's success. The person with codependency issues may also feel resentment when their loved one fails to be grateful for their help and compassion.

Over time, narcissists learn how to exploit and manipulate their partners' people-pleasing tendencies for their own supply. As their sense of self-

worth is becoming inflated, this person may make large demands for more attention and resources from their partner, leading to a breaking point.
Although the relationship may not be healthy, many people find themselves unable to leave. They are afraid to be alone. Outside of help, this dynamic can grow more and more toxic.

When Is the Overlap Pathological?

The literature discussing the difference between codependency and narcissistic relationships is sparse. However, pathological narcissism begins with a profound lack of empathy or impairments in one's ability to recognize other's feelings and needs, while in codependent relationships.
The interplay of codependency and narcissism truly becomes pathological when they undermine another's quality of life or cause them to do harm.

The Codependent Empath

If you are a reader who identifies as an empath, you might also be inclined to be a codependent. Empaths are natural caretakers and healers and they are compassionate people who struggle with imbalance and are always seeking to help even when it is inappropriate. As an empath, you are highly sensitive but it is your values that make you so easily targeted by narcissists.

Codependents and empaths do have distinct characteristics. By contrast, empaths are strongly empathetic and very good at understanding others' emotions. They are also sensitive to sound, touch and other people's feelings. They are someone with a rich inner world and because of that, his or her nervous system gets easily drawn into social stimuli.

Codependency, however, is a more specific condition. Codependents are constantly focused on the needs of others and have a hard time turning down a plea to help someone else. They are often preoccupied with enabling, pleasing, or defending. Their focus is solely on someone else and how that person is feeling, without really being able to fully empathize with them.

So what classifies as a codependent empath?

Codependent empaths are people with two major predicaments: while they are sensitive to others, they have difficulty protecting themselves and may be vulnerable to more abuse due to their inability to create boundaries. They are highly sensitive to other people while having blurred boundaries between themselves and others.

Recovery as a codependent empath begins with recognizing that empathy is a double-edged sword. You become more sensitive to other people's emotions and yet you feel the need to save them from their feelings of pain. This might mean trying to avoid the feelings in yourself or choosing to focus on other people's emotions instead of your own. True recovery starts with being aware of your own needs and feelings. Don't turn away from the pain you feel. Instead, show compassion for this part of yourself as you would be a highly sensitive person. Although this is especially important for empaths, it is a good practice to help you differentiate your emotions and honor yourself.

Overcoming The Codependent Narcissist Trap

Many codependents refuse to end the unhealthy relationship because it would seem like a personal failure and show them as defective. Remember, the codependent's goal is to save the relationship, not end it. The codependent feels they have a right to be in the narcissist's life. They fear that going away would create abandonment and inevitably lead to the end of the relationship. Thus, it's not uncommon to see a codependent being very provocative in hopes of forcing an abandonment crisis. In fact, this is often why they cannot leave the narcissist – they don't want to cause abandonment.

The cycle for a codependent starts with being liked to falling out of favor and trying to gain back the affection. The codependent is always trying to recapture the high they felt when they first started dating. The excitement, however, never comes back because it was never real to begin with.

A codependent person can give a narcissist the supply they need, which usually comes through attention and validation. They provide it for two main reasons: admiration and to regulate their emotions and self-worth. This never-ending cycle of approval and disapproval leaves no room for effective problem solving.

This leads to a revolving pattern of behaviors where both narcissists and codependents suffer long-term consequences. There is an unspoken agreement that both parties are too scared and too hurt to actually work on their unresolved childhood wounds. The narcissist's false self needs a constant supply and the codependent works to avoid conflict and criticism. When the cycle ends, it is likely because the narcissist moves on to a newer, more inviting supply and will abandon the relationship.

After a narcissist has left a codependent, one of the ways a person can begin to heal is by addressing self-esteem issues or depression they might be having.

Setting Boundaries After The Cycle Has Ended

Leaving a codependent narcissist means that you need to learn how to love and protect yourself, and stand firm on your own feet. You need to learn your personal value and worth. You must adopt effective self-love practices. The following steps are critical for overcoming codependency with a narcissist.

1. Initiate Awareness

Start by becoming aware of how you feel. You should ask yourself, are there any indications you're unhappy and if so, what are the reasons? The important thing to understand is if you are paying attention to you own needs.

2. Observe Yourself Without Judgment

The second step is to look at your behavior, without any judgment. Watch the way you behave around others, including your friends. If a friend is fixing a meal and asks you what you would like, do you say, "I don't care, whatever you want is okay" or do you have a definite answer? If you have been part of the codependent narcissist trap, you are likely needing practice in active assertiveness.

Being clear and diligently prioritizing your preferences will allow you to work towards a goal of having more balanced relationships, as boundaries can only be drawn when you know what they are. When you do not reveal your preferences, desires or needs to the people around you, you stop yourself from being known. Doing so will allow for more closeness with the people in your life.

3. Assert Yourself In Safe Zones

Start being more assertive around people you trust. At the next get-together, tell your friend what you really want for lunch, and they may give it to you. Being assertive around safe people also allows you to become accustomed to saying 'no' to others and building your boundary muscles.

4. Start Speaking Up In All Social Areas

The fourth step is to make your voice heard. Decide on what you want and stand up for it. You can use simple, nonaggressive communication to start asserting yourself.

Some people that suffer from codependency may be uncertain about how to begin a boundary request, but starting with a positive sentiment can make it easier. You can say things such as "Thanks for offering to drive. I really appreciate it, but I can't make it to the beach this weekend because I promised to help my aunt move" or "That sounds fun, but I really need to catch up on some work."

As you learn to express your feelings, desires, priorities and expectations more openly, others do hear what you are saying.

Recovering from the codependent narcissist trap requires changing an internal dialogue that is often negative about the self and beating yourself up for "what could have been". This feeds into the toxic victim narrative that is common after a narcissistic relationship ends. You might find yourself telling yourself "I should have done this" or "how could I have missed that?". Stop. These thoughts are erroneous and will sabotage your recovery by making you feel worse and more determined to go back into the relationship.

With the practical steps provided in this section, your internal dialogue will change and you'll start celebrating your recovery successes every day. In the next chapter, we are going to learn how to conquer enabling behavior.

Chapter 3. How To Stop Enabling Others

Codependency is often characterized by denial. You live a reality distorted from what it actually is – often at the expense of your own self-interest. Codependents do not want to change, and it's likely because they're being cushioned by those around them who are accepting of their behavior. They deny their destructive behavior, which causes them to endure detrimental consequences and painful relationships. A codependent will usually cover up their true feelings and needs. This will put off true acceptance of the situation.

Pretending something doesn't bother us prevents us from taking the necessary steps to fix it. Those with codependency issues refuse to give up control, even when facts are against them. They get angry when people don't behave the way they expect them to. However, the truth is they will never be able to change other people and should instead focus on changing themselves through living the life they want.

Codependents have a hard time letting go, in part because of their own anxiety and discomfort in the face of changes that are not within their control. When codependents finally begin to let go, they feel a lot of anxiety and depression. They recognize for the first time what their attempts at control have been trying to conceal, such as loneliness and anxiety about making necessary changes. True recovery from codependency involves acknowledging our limitations, accepting that we are powerless in some things, and accepting the limitations of others.

The first step to accepting people for who they are involves letting go of all your illusions about who they could or should be. This means you should stop expecting people to behave in accordance with your desires, values, or taste. If they do something that surprises you, it is never because they did it to make you mad or hurt you in any way. This is key. Think back on the most negative reactions you have ever had towards somebody else for their beliefs and ask yourself what you were really trying to do. I would bet you that the real answer is that deep down inside, underneath all of your righteous outrage, lies a desire to fix that person. To show them that by finally doing the right thing, they will finally be happy. To make them fix what is "wrong" with them and get on board with your way of thinking. It is the belief that anyone acting in a way contrary to your desires has it wrong and if they could just see the light, they would see what they are missing out on. If they could just open their eyes, they would realize how happy they could be with what you have to offer.

The problem with this approach is that it presumes you know better than the person involved as to what will make them happy. Whether they come to this conclusion on their own, with your help or not, your constant judgment and benevolence does not permit them a chance to grow into their own person and find their own happiness. It's akin to a rescuer attitude-- someone always knows what's best. They find themselves obsessed with someone and unable to let go. Rather than nurturing and caring for themselves, they subjugate their whole selves and lose their identity.

Letting Go of Enabling Behavior

When you obsess over a person or judge them, try to detach and question your motives. Can you honestly control their feelings and behavior? Letting go requires a shift in consciousness, and a repeated effort to not focus on the problem. If you worry or over think too much, you are limited in the way you can live your life.

Here are some practical steps to put an end to being an enabler:

1. Detach or Create Physical Distance

Understanding the power of detachment is important when obsessing over a person or situation. When we separate or remove ourselves from the person or event that is giving us stress, this decreases our emotional investment to what is occurring. As we create this distance, we are more mentally capable of letting go.

2. Create Positive Mantras Against Negative Thoughts

When things go wrong in your life and you're faced with painful emotions, it can be helpful to have a reminder that helps you reframe your thoughts. Having a mantra that you tell yourself during times of pain and suffering can help change how you think about your situation.

Mantras are an effective tool for codependents to overcome anxiety and negative thinking. If used properly, a mantra can encourage reflection and redirect attention away from unhelpful behaviors. Positive mantras for breaking away from codependent behaviors include saying:

- "I am better than my addiction"
- "I deserve to break free"
- "I am in control of my own happiness"
- "I deserve the best"

Recite these affirmations to yourself regularly. As a codependent, reciting positive statements can be helpful in lessening anxiety. Take some time to reflect on kind and loving words you can say to yourself in order to help you shed the shame and self- blame often associated with detaching from others. If you tend to get caught up in feeling guilty or responsible for another person, especially your addicted or hurtful loved ones, use the following phrases to release feelings of guilt and avoid adding more guilt to your equation:

- "I am not responsible for hurting or addicted people"
- "I am not responsible for another person's behavior, choices or feelings"

After adopting the right affirmations, you will get accustomed to viewing a situation in a more rational light when there is absolutely nothing you can do to help the person. Detaching yourself in a healthy, willing way from enabling and codependency behavior will allow you to let go and move on.

3. Engage in Self Care

When learning to let go of enabling patterns, the practice of self-care is the best tool a person can have. Because the majority of codependents are self-sacrificial, self-care is about having a higher self worth and knowing that you deserve the best for yourself. By making time for self-care, you can also feel a greater sense of autonomy.

Lay out some ground rules for your self-care practice. Maybe it's time away from other members of your household, like going to the park, or doing something special for yourself alone. Allow yourself guilt-free "you time." Take a bath without being interrupted, watch TV or just sit and visit with a pet. Pray for yourself, not only when you are in intense emotional distress, but also just to affirm who you are-- God's beloved. Treat yourself as you would a friend or family member who needs care taking, and decide how often a good practice for self-care is for you. Think about what normal, daily living may look like for you--and then gradually fit those activities within your lifestyle.

Write out your new schedule and place it where you can see it. By giving yourself positive encouragement throughout the day, you will help yourself avoid the need to be dependent.

4. Write Down Your Feelings

Journaling is an effective practice in codependency recovery. This process enables you to reflect on your thoughts and formulate new methodical ideas of how to handle instances that may normally send you into avoidance behavior and negative thinking. Focusing on the positive ways in which you want to grow as a person and ways you can counteract your negative tendencies is the most effective. Plan to journal daily. You may want to begin each entry with a mood scale rating, followed by an honest assessment of how you are feeling. Examples include:

- If I were to evaluate how excited I am right now, on a scale from 1-10 with ten being the most excited, how would I rate my mood?

- If I were to evaluate how calm and relaxed I am right now, on a scale from 1-10 with ten being the most relaxed, how would I rate my mood?
- What am I obsessing about right now? Is it a person or an event?
- How many times did I obsess about this person or event?

If you find that you are truly obsessed over someone, journaling will show the obsession's pattern. You can also ask yourself the following:

- Were there any interruptions during the periods of time I obsessed over this person?
- Did these interruptions break the cyclic obsessive cycle?
- When did I start obsessing?

Keep monitoring your mood in a journal. Awareness of any patterns plus awareness of your emotional state will assist you with changing.

5. Learn to Relax

Since codependents are so busy attending to others, they often struggle to relax. They become either too busy or so exhausted that relaxation is definitely not something they do on a regular basis. However, relaxation is an important part of self -care. If you are too busy, scattered, and stressed out to even think about relaxing, daily self-care is going to be even more difficult for you to create.

A useful way to start relaxing is gradually increasing your activity, such as walking or working around the yard after dinner. Slowly increase the amount of time you spend on daily, relaxing activities so you begin to build peaceful memories around being physically active. Spending one hour a week watching TV or going on an hour-long walk around the neighborhood are initial goals you can set to begin your relaxation journey.

6. Be Present And Accepting of Your Feelings

When we are mindful and come into the now, we're able to tap back into our power source. When you're in the present and not focused on a "problem" or person, your perspective grows opposite from that narrow view.

Codependents need to focus on the present to help assess their current situation or feelings. For many people, this is very challenging. Some may use distractions to block out painful feelings. These include drinking, drugs, workaholism or overeating. Some may make themselves physically sick to distract from their emotions. Distractions also include accompanying or enabling others who are engaging in harmful behaviors. When you focus on the present, many of these distractions will no longer work. This is why many codependents fear living in the present, because they know without these distractions they may be forced to face uncomfortable situations.

Learn to notice your emotions and feelings when they are happening. Learning to simply be in the moment with yourself and identifying your current feelings and surroundings is a good way to begin. You'll be able to make corrections in your behavior and how you react to things as they occur. It's also very important in the healing process to learn how to change codependent patterns that have worked in your life. Use the following questions to reflect on the present moment:

- Am I calm or stressed?
- What thoughts are going through my head right now?
- Does my body feel tight or tense?

Through this process, you'll begin to get out of your head and into your heart.

7. Engage in the Serenity Prayer

Many people who don't pray every day may not think of asking for help. The act of surrender allows the ego to let go of their attachment to the problem and release the mental blockage that is preventing us from moving forwards. Praying is very effective for accepting what you can't change, especially in regards to other people.

The Serenity Prayer is particularly effective in helping you process your feelings and clear the fog of codependency. It helps you release your grip on another person or circumstance. The prayer can be repeated out loud:

> "God, grant me the serenity to accept the things I cannot change, courage to change the things I can, and the wisdom to know the difference."

Mindsets To Break the Pattern of Enabling Others

Codependents usually have a feeling of emptiness and low self- worth, which causes them to focus on others and only see the positives about the other person. They may devote time, effort, attention, money and resources to everyone else without being returned with the love and attention that they need and desire. It is easy for a codependent to become an enabler to his or her own self-destructive friends or family. Enabling can be seen as a way for the codependent to distance themselves from intimate relations. It gives them the illusion that they are going to control, fix or change their loved one's behavior as well as their own.

Enabling behaviors, such as codependents providing their loved ones with money, also help to reduce outside interaction in their interpersonal relationships. Enabling is a way of protecting people that they love from seeing them for who they actually are. Relying upon enabling hinders the relationship and reveals negative attitudes on the part of the dependent person. In discussing enabling, it is important to address that many enablers have their own issues and needs that they are not addressing, such as past experiences with dysfunctional relationships or any form of prior abuse.

The question, "Can a codependent break the pattern of enabling?" requires time spent on self-reflection. In order to change their dysfunctional patterns, they need to address the root of their codependency and change their behavior. Although the process is arduous when dealing with a loved one, a codependent can take steps to put an end to this behavior. In no particular order, the following strategies will allow the codependent to break their own negative enabling pattern.

1. **Let Others Learn For Themselves**

    Learn to give others responsibility so they can make their own decisions. Let them experience both success and failure in order to grow. Maintain appropriate boundaries in order to have a firm sense of self and acknowledge that you don't need to take care of everyone.

2. **Tolerate Uncertainty**

    One of the most important things for you to do is to learn to live with uncertainty. Allow yourself to feel the anxiety that comes when you don't know, or can't control what others do. And when you can actually let go and trust that life is happening the way it's happening, a new level of peace will follow. Trust that things won't always happen as you want them to…this is the journey of life. Accept the unknown and allow for events that you don't understand.

    Codependents want to do things their way; they want to control others and situations. They can often appear as over-achievers from the outside, but are unable to achieve their own personal desired results because they lack the appropriate skills to put forth the effort required. Even when things go right in their lives, they can't enjoy them fully.

3. **Make Self Improvements**

    You must focus on developing yourself and understanding your fears and weaknesses, while working to make changes that are good for you and your family. Stop focusing on others and work on making personal improvements that will eventually pay off positively in your life. Develop a realistic sense of self and you will learn to gain your own trust. When you know who you are, it's easier to not care so much about what others think.

4. Accept That Others Will Change Over Time

You must be willing to accept that other people will change – and things will always be uncertain. It may take a long time, but it is part of the process. You cannot rush it or control it. Your loved ones must learn to trust themselves and treat others with respect, even if they sometimes fail.

5. Accept That Your Old Behaviors Were Dysfunctional

Accept that you might find the old negative behaviors more comfortable because they put control in your hands while deciding everything for other people. Mourn the times when you felt like you were in control of someone. Embrace the freedom of others making their own decisions. Look forward to your loved ones celebrating the successes in their lives so they will no longer need you to take away pain.

Codependency recovery means fighting the tendency to go back to old habits when your loved ones make mistakes.

6. Pace Yourself

Focus on taking it easy and pacing your actions rather than feeling like you have to do everything by yourself. When it comes to self-reliance, pacing is key to avoid burnout and anxiety. Keeping your stress levels down will help keep your mind and body strong. Stress can cause fatigue and panic, so keep your head in the game by confronting your anxieties and accepting uncertainty with a healthy outlook.

Before you know it, you'll be able to trust yourself. You will experience a sense of inner calm knowing that you don't have to rely on another person's approval.

7. Believe That You Are On A New Journey

Understand that new behaviors are changing how you act and handle yourself, with new ways of relating to others. You are on the road to letting go of enabling behaviors. You will notice that you are feeling good about staying in boundaries, and not making excuses for others, or taking responsibility when they don't. New behavior may stir up guilt, anger or panic, as you doing what is best for yourself. You will, however, adjust and see that your boundaries in helping others are healthy and compassionate.

8. Realize That We Only Grow Through Struggle

Life is difficult, but if we are able to find ways to face our struggles, and try new things, we can become more developed as a person. Through struggle and experiences, we find out who we really are. This can become extremely frightening, or exhilarating. Whether you've ventured out of your comfort zone, or stepped in to help too much, any growth that comes through pain should be embraced as an opportunity.

9. Accept That Being An Enabler Is An Addictive Behavior

As an enabler, you are often addicted to helping the ones you care for but it's important to be aware that by doing so, you also help enable your own addiction. This results in both of you getting worse. Admitting that your own behavior is dangerous, like your loved one's, is a critical step in recovery.

10. Commit To Positive Behavior When Relating To Others

Always remember that all of your behaviors should involve you. You must ask yourself, however, if you want these behaviors to be positive or negative. Enabling ends up damaging both the enabler and the individual with the addiction. Allow your loved one to learn from their experience and recognize their own mistakes.

11. Learn To Celebrate Change and Growth

Celebrate the chance to grow, even when things are difficult. One part of healing from codependency is to begin to make choices that are good and healthy for you. Stop thinking of yourself as a bad person simply because you aren't all things to all people. Although codependency is intertwined with intimacy issues, you may begin to discover that as you learn more about yourself, you experience a greater sense of authenticity.

12. Accept That You Don't "Need To Be Needed"

Learn to just be yourself and stop trying to be needed all the time. You will end up being exhausted if you are always an enabler or helper. Dealing with the guilt of enabling often makes codependents very angry inside. Hurt and pain are actually your loved one's feelings, not yours. Realize that you are allowing another person's behavior to sabotage your own happiness.

Enablers need to let go of their need to save others and not make excuses for why they need to help them continuously. Codependency recovery begins when you start to break the pattern of thinking you know what is best for others.

Living in the midst of any type of addiction can put you in depression, feeling hopeless and full of fear. Learning to abandon enabling behavior is a powerful step toward recovery. Being able to let go of these habits allows you to regain your power. In the next chapter, we are going to discuss the practical aspects of communication and how to be more assertive when overcoming codependency.

Chapter 4. Communication Styles

Communication is vital to life or else we are disadvantaged. There are many issues that codependents have with communicating. A lot of the time, they lack awareness and end up in a power struggle. This leads them to exhibit poor boundaries and unhealthy attachment patterns to others. If you are a codependent then you probably struggle to communicate with others as effectively as you should. It's possible that you don't realize that there is an issue or any reasons why it's happening.

Codependents often struggle to understand the messages they are sending and receiving. Communication from a codependent to an addict can be passive aggressive, enabling or even child-like. This is a coping mechanism that eventually breaks down the relationship. They don't want to make waves and would rather play everything safe.

Assertive vs. Aggressive Communication

Two ways of communicating that can be mistaken as one another are assertive and aggressive. Assertiveness is characterized by the capability to express your opinion or point of view without it impeding on the rights of others. It's about being confident in your own skin, even if that means expressing disagreement. On the other hand, aggression is about exerting pressure on another person's rights for what you want. It's about force and is always based on fear of rejection. Fear makes you aggressive because it hinders you from showing assertiveness.

When you're still in the process of learning to interpret what assertive communication is, it can be easy to mistake it for something that's aggressive. Aggressive communication is more likely to include things like yelling, name-calling, being sarcastic (as a way to insult the other person), and even threatening physical harm or legal action.

However, being assertive means you are firm and direct when you say something. An assertive person is totally in charge of who he or she is. The key to being assertive is to be positive, respectful and genuine with yourself and others.

That being said, avoidance, hostility, criticism, anger and other negative behavior can sometimes be contained within an assertive manner of communicating. Therefore, the line between aggressive and assertive can be a matter of small degree. Sometimes being aggressive can be justifiable (for example, if it is used for self-defense). Sometimes you may even need to be aggressive while performing some difficult teamwork tasks just to help others be more assertive – who wouldn't want that? But again, we cannot avoid the fact that aggression can be very destructive if misused or inappropriately applied.

In the end, assertive communication usually helps people succeed without getting into an unpleasant scene or creating problems with their relationships.

Overcoming Codependent Communication Patterns

All people should have the right to speak their mind. Negative emotions and thoughts are necessary. Communication is a fundamental human need. Not being able to express oneself is equivalent to lacking one of the senses. All of the following patterns discussed in this section are just a few learned behaviors. They can be unlearned, too.

The communication of codependents is often incomplete. This leads to misunderstandings and resentments. Codependents need to work on becoming more self-aware so that they can improve their communication strategies for more effective and healthy relationships in the future.

Here is a list of communication patterns typical of codependents, along with ways to overcome them:

Avoidance or Lazy Communication

Texting or email is a common way of delivering difficult messages from codependents because it avoids the confrontation. Codependents avoid face to face or telephone communication, because they fear confronting an issue right then and there.

The best way to communicate is to talk openly and face your issues. If you tend to avoid it and communicate indirectly, stop. Treat other people with respect and be frank about the details.

Taking Too Much Responsibility

When there is a conflict or a dispute, it is common for those who are codependent to take responsibility for something they did not do. It's easier for a codependent to take the blame than to try standing up for themselves.

In communication, if you want to stop taking blame for others, you can replace the word "I" and "you" with "we" and place these words in front of your statement. This recalibrates the conversation to the other person. For example:

- Instead of saying, "I don't understand what you're asking," try saying "We have a problem listening to each other."
- Instead of saying, "I'm sorry for not paying more attention to you," try saying, "We don't pay enough attention to how we speak to each other."
- Instead of saying "I am going to keep the house more clean," try saying, "We need to work out a system for keeping our house clean."

Being a Pleaser

Codependents struggle with saying 'no' to people. They'll take care of others even when it causes them to suffer. They will go to any length, even sacrificing themselves, in order to avoid disappointing anyone. Being a people pleaser can be destructive to an individual. Sure, you sometimes get the benefits of being a nice person, but it usually turns out that other people will just take advantage of your kindness and give nothing back in return.

If you are a people pleaser all time, these are the best ideas that can help you to stop being one. First, learn how to firmly say 'No'. Next time somebody makes requests, answer them with a polite refusal in your voice. You could say things like, "I'd love to go but I can't, sorry!" or "That is outside of my job description".

Avoidant or Deflection

A codependent can be afraid of getting hurt or blamed. They will avoid any possible conflict and pretend that things are fine, pretending that the problems aren't happening. They will avoid the topic of contention completely, even if it causes more harm.

A codependent might think that, as long as they take care of the people in their lives and solve all their problems, there won't be any room for conflict. But conflict is a built-in part of any relationship. Overcoming avoidance is accomplished by dropping our defenses and acknowledging vulnerabilities and needs. What we need is not avoidance of pain, but the courage to accept it and work through it.

Deflecting is an avoidance technique that people use when they don't know what to say, want to push responsibility away, or avoid being confronted about something. You may have learned to deflect as a way of coping with uncomfortable moments, disputes and disagreements. Codependents will try to dismiss and reject the confrontation of anything they don't want to deal with. They will attempt to change the topic of the conversation as quickly as possible. Overcoming deflection can be achieved by addressing the situation head on.

It is best to adopt the practice of using clarifying statements during conflict. Examples include responding with the follow:

- "What do you mean?"
- "How did this come about?"
- "I don't know, guide me through what led up to this issue."

- "What were you trying to tell me?
- "If there is a problem, please share it."

By addressing a dispute directly, avoiding deflection prevents the consequence of bottled anger and resentment commonly experienced by codependents.

Indecision

When pressured to do something they don't want to, a codependent will often stall or try to put it off for the time being. Instead of giving a direct answer, they will give vague replies. They are often afraid of setting boundaries with others and come off as people-pleasers. This may lead their friends and family members to feel confused, frustrated, and sometimes put off when they lack directness.

Being more decisive starts with practice. When presented with a request, use affirmative statements like:

- "I'm sorry, but I have other plans this weekend."
- "I am swamped and can't take on any more responsibilities."
- "I am sorry to hear you are upset, but I will not be taking on any more commitments."
- Or simply, "I can't do that. I am sorry."

By overcoming common communication mistakes, codependents can finally face their emotions directly instead of using unhealthy ways to cope.

Assertiveness Training

Communication plays such a vital role in our lives that it determines whether or not a relationship can survive. It is vital for success and reflects your level of self-esteem to others. Being assertive in your communication will command respect, project confidence, and inspire others to do the same. This type of speaking is courteous. It encourages honest, direct, open discussion that's respectful and non-threatening.

Communication skills are learned by experience, and with practice can help you with your self-esteem and improve your overall relationships. Codependent people often have a hard time establishing boundaries between themselves and their loved ones. By nature, codependents are more likely to be passive-aggressive rather than being assertive as it is normal for them to take on the stress of others.

Here are the most effective techniques to improve assertiveness:

Make Clear Statements

One of the hardest things about codependence is being able to be assertive and vocal about what you need. This can feel completely terrifying because you fear rejection, criticism, or even anger from those in your close circles. Learn how to speak up and make clear statements. When you are codependent, it's important to be direct and straightforward. You should make a statement of what you need, think or feel in a clear way. This includes using "I" statements such as:

- "I am not capable to make that commitment right now."
- "I am unhappy about how this was handled."
- "I feel scared right now."
- "I need you to say that you are sorry for what happened.

When put into practice, simple statements such as these lead to greater self-awareness and overcoming fear of rejection.

Have Congruent Body Language

One of the things that codependents struggle with is body language. They are often misread or interpreted as being mean, rude, or angry. The problem is that they don't know what their natural position should be. Body language is a powerful and instinctual human behavior. The things that you do with your body, say far more than anything your mouth could say. In fact, everything in your body can affect the message you're trying to convey without knowing it.

Congruence is an important concept in body language. If your words and actions don't match, people will not be able to accept the message. For instance, imagine someone telling you how they are happy as they walk away from you with a slouched posture and non-expressive face.

Your body language won't be in alignment with your posture if you don't have a strong, confident stance. This will make your posture and words look more incongruent when speaking assertively. When communicating, try to show the other person that you care by smiling during the conversation. Be aware of how tense your body language is while doing so.

Many times when a person is trying to have congruent body language, they forget to take deep breaths and on many occasions this is the calming signal they are missing in their habits or mannerisms. If you want to have emotional congruence and constant eye contact with someone while conversing, then try to mirror their posture. You can use segments of your own body to show attention and engagement with the other person. We tend to move into higher levels of tension when people threaten our egos, confidence or integrity. To correct low self-esteem your goal might be to notice non-verbally when the tension is going down in your body.

Be More Concise When Speaking

Speech is more impactful the shorter it is. Your listener wants you to get right to the point, so you need to keep it short. When you beat around the bush, it tells a person you aren't sure of what you are doing. Vague language is rooted in insecurity or lack of knowledge.

If you fear speaking up, start by addressing the root cause of this fear. Next, practice what you'll say out loud and anticipate how others will react. It's a good idea to let people know what you want at the beginning of any sentence.

Be A Better Listener

A good listener is someone who is focused and attentive to the speaker and understands their feelings. It shows that you are a supportive person, but as codependents it can be challenging to dip into this mode of listening. As codependents we are so prone to take on the feelings of the other person that we often start venting or advising them about what they should do with their situation.

It can be difficult to shut up and allow them to talk their feelings out. This sounds simple but is a challenge for codependents. There are a few questions to ask yourself to progress in listening:

- Are you being supportive or sympathetic? Sympathy involves agreeing with the person or reassuring them that everything will be okay.
- Are you listening with care?
- Instead of fixing their situation, are you allowing them to talk and feeling without giving advice?
- Are you accepting of whatever they say and not discounting their thoughts, words or feelings? (This is hard for codependents who tend to judge people's words and feelings as right or wrong, superior or inferior).

Allow yourself to get out of your own head and into other people's thought processes. It takes effort, patience and practice. When you try listening with compassionate curiosity, you may surprise yourself in how well it relaxes you and your friends. Cognizance of others is essential. To be heard, you must first listen. The key to good communication is listening, paying attention, and showing respect when others speak.

Claim Ownership of Your Thoughts, Feels and Needs

You have a responsibility to yourself. This means accepting your opinions, thoughts, feelings, and needs without shifting the responsibility onto others. When you express your opinions, other people are less inclined to defend and justify their positions because you will just be talking about yourself. However, this is more challenging when you are emotional. You should wait and think about your feelings and desired changes before talking with the person.

Claiming your thoughts and feelings is the first step in taking ownership of your life. As a codependent, it is something that has to occur in order for you to feel better about yourself.

Be Courteous

The purpose of assertive communication is to share feelings and thoughts, not to vent. Being discourteous to the listener will lose their interest quickly. You need to engage with your listener to be effective. Constructive criticism delivered assertively is more likely to be paid attention to.

When you're speaking to someone, it's important that you take their thoughts into account and make them feel at ease. There are a lot of ways to do this, like giving the person some space, asking if they're okay every once in awhile, and avoiding arguments.

It is important to take a moment and listen to the other person have their say. Find out what they are trying to express, and then in a timely manner, give them some of their space. While it may not be necessary, a courteous response can go a long way. You will be giving them some room to feel how they need to feel, instead of reacting in kind with your fear and anger.

Non Passive Aggressive Assertiveness Techniques

One of the key steps to overcoming assertiveness is truly understanding what being assertive means and being able to communicate in that style. Active communication assumes mutual respect. In other words, we will still respect the person even if they do or say something we don't like. This style of communicating comes from the idea that people should be treated with respect even when they are acting poorly.

- **Learn How To Say "No"… While Avoiding Guilt**

It's ok to say 'no' from time to time. Believe it or not, people would actually respect you more for your honesty and autonomous decision-making skills. In fact, being assertive doesn't have to be a difficult task at all. Practice saying 'no' to your friends until you get good at it. It can be hard to give up and turn down just any opportunity, when you think of all the reasons that convince you to say 'yes'.

- **Open Ended Questioning**

It's important to listen actively to what people are trying to say, and this will often show you how someone is feeling. If you maintain a calm and curious attitude, things will often get resolved much quicker than they would otherwise. Being very careful with questions is a way to make assertive communication. This means asking open-ended questions and avoiding assumptions. Ideas that seem obvious to some may not be to others.

You are communicating on a conscious level when you are assertive. You can control the conversation, satisfying your needs, instead of always reacting to other people's words. You can ask open-ended questions that require more than a simple yes or no answer. Open ended questions such as what, how, where, when can reveal their hidden thoughts. Closed ended questions such as 'yes' or 'no' cannot be answered in many different ways and can lead you to misinterpretation and an ineffective conversation.

Asking a well-thought out, open-ended question can be the first step in establishing some personal boundaries. Codependents have difficulty setting and maintaining limits on others. If you are feeling this way, you can ask questions like:

- "What would you say we should do about the issue?"
- "Ok, so what are some of your thoughts on that?"
- "If you don't mind me asking, what are your reasons for thinking that might be the case?"
- "What do you have in mind about how we can address this problem?"

- **Let Go Of Frequent Guilt**

Doing something difficult can make you feel guilty, but who does that really help? Imagine the situation that's making you feel bad about your actions. Were your actions really wrong? If so, can they be changed? If not, focus on building a life that improves. Guilt often holds people back and does not help in any way.

Giving up guilt is an important aspect of assertiveness. Codependents often feel guilty for taking anything they please in order to improve their own life. The only way to overcome this is by letting go of the actual guilt. To put this into practice, you must question if you need to feel guilty in the first place. When a situation arises, you can do this by asking yourself any of the following:

- How is this my responsibility?
- Is my guilt enabling others?
- By saying 'yes', do others avoid responsibility?
- By saying 'yes', will I allow the other person to resolve his or her own problems?

This is not an easy process but focusing on shame and guilt reduces overall enjoyment of life. Feelings of joy are the most helpful for dealing with low self-esteem. Opinions are like noses, everybody has one. That means that you are better off concentrating on your own feelings and thoughts than other people's. When a problem arises, pay attention to what you feel rather than what you think.

Guilt can deter our lives in a negative way, but when we let go, we are setting ourselves free from the chains that limit us.

- **Know Your Needs And Wants... Then Ask For It**

If you never consider your own needs or desires, how can you go about asking for them? Prior to affirming your needs when communicating with others, you might need to do some extensive research on your part to know exactly what you want.

You might be too preoccupied with the needs of others, which in turn has burdened you. Use this moment to brainstorm what you want and need. Don't be afraid to express your feelings because it's the only way that you can prioritize yourself.

Let's say, for example, you're talking to your boss about a promotion. You know that you deserve it. And even if they don't have any openings currently available for someone with your new skill set, you can make sure that the conversation leads to a conversation on future opportunities. Instead of always expecting your boss to read your mind and know what would be an appropriate time to ask for a raise, you need to communicate what you want.

By using active steps you will be more likely to convince your boss that you are deserving of one based on your performance.

- **Taking Your Time**

People may put pressure on you and make you feel stressed about making a decision while you are not ready. It can be difficult to make a decision when the stakes are high and you don't have all of the facts. One of the most significant lessons you can learn is that when you're a codependent, you should always take your time to respond. This will decrease anxiety and unnecessary stress that should be placed on other individuals when you need help.

You reserve the right to think things through before making a decision. The following phrases may seem simple at first, but can be difficult for a codependent struggling to embrace their individuality in the moment.

- "Sorry, I need to check my schedule before I can get back to you."
- "I need more time to think about this. How about we schedule a follow up meeting this week?"
- "I'll get back to you as soon as possible."

- **Broken Record**

A "broken record" technique is helpful in cases where people try to bully you into making a difficult decision without considering anything you have said. This is the best assertiveness technique of them all and it is exactly what you would think it is -- you simply keep repeating your stance, regardless of what the other person says.

The broken record technique uses persistence to re-state your message in order to change people's minds and behaviors. For example, if you are being asked for money, repeat the phrase, "I know I've given money to you in the past, but I am unable to do it any longer." Or in a work scenario, "I have too much work on my plate to extend myself any further."

As childlike as it might seem, this technique is highly effective in disrupting long-term codependent behaviors.

- **Fogging Technique**

Fogging is an assertiveness tactic used to disarm a person and it can be used in a variety of different ways. To start, you find a truth that the other person will agree is correct and then you continue to make your point. At work, for example, since you both agree that there is immense pressure for the team to meet a quota, you reiterate that you both need to stay on top of your designated tasks and that you cannot handle assuming any part of someone else's responsibilities. Or if there is a problem with household spending, you and your partner both agree that excessive spending needs to stop, after which you then propose a monthly budget.

Practice these skills while imagining different scenarios. Consider how the other person is likely to respond. How can you reply assertively? If you feel you should have been more assertive in a situation, review the experience without judgment. Practice what you would say if it happened again until you feel comfortable talking about it.

- **"I" Messaging**

A lot of people think that the way to be assertive is to tell the other person what they're doing wrong and why it's wrong, but that kind of language typically creates more problems than it fixes. One of the things that codependents need to learn how to do is be assertive, and in order to do so, they should know how to use "I" messages out loud. When you want to express how you feel about someone's behavior, avoid "you" messages and replace them with positive "I" messages.

There are many reasons why codependents need to use "I" messaging, but one of the more important reasons is because a codependent needs to focus less on what other people want or expect from them. "I" messages promote accountability and taking responsibility for the problems at hand. They also acknowledge coping strategies, something that co-dependents often deal with daily. People who use "I" messages are more likely to set realistic and necessary boundaries, such as acknowledging responsibility for a particular behavior.

There is a big difference between "I" messaging and "you" messaging. The majority of the problems in relationships are caused by the use of the word "you." If we describe something that happened, he or she may take it like they're being reprimanded, criticized or blamed. "I" messages are usually described as assertive communication. They always look at a certain situation and help clarify behavior by giving feedback or responsibility.

For instance saying, "I want you to stop taking so much of my time," is much better than, "You never spend any time with me."

Another good example is, "I find you disrespectful when you never do what I ask...", as opposed to, "You are so controlling."

When "I" messaging is used properly, it reinforces responsibility, yet holds people accountable.

Embracing more assertive communication behaviors and overcoming negative habits will allow you to gain a new perspective on life and improve your level of self-worth. In the next chapter, we will discuss the practice of setting healthy and effective boundaries.

Chapter 5. How To Set Boundaries

Setting boundaries as a codependent can seem daunting. When you set boundaries with someone who is emotionally dependent on you, it can feel like you're depriving them from getting what they need, or even worse it might feel like you are rejecting them. However, in an unhealthy relationship this kind of neglect leads to more conflict and more pain for both parties in the long-term.

Not setting boundaries can cause you a lot of frustration and resentment, which might start to show sooner or later. One of the first things you must do before setting boundaries is to take an honest assessment of your triggers. Commonly, these are identified as either internal or external.

Codependency triggers can show us what we believe deep inside by how they make us react. When we are threatened, this shows we still have more to learn about ourselves and our situations. Once we recognize the trigger as a defense mechanism, we can become aware of the deeper beliefs and emotions lying beneath. This allows us to become mindful of how these emotions affect our reactions and allow us to make healthier choices.

Often, when we're codependent in romantic relationships, we don't see it. We don't realize it because on the surface, it seems like this relationship looks like all the other ones. If you suffered with codependency since childhood (you may have an abusive, alcoholic parent which can perpetuate codependency as well), much of what has influenced you has now been normalized into your behavior. Oftentimes we don't even recognize what is right in front of our eyes.

Internal Triggers

Everybody has that voice inside them telling them they are not good enough. This inner critic is formed by learned beliefs that are not healthy, often leading to shame if they are not maintained. You may feel triggered when you think you're being selfish, which can cause you to offer help to someone that might be harmful to yourself. One of the many ways in which people are fooled into cognitive dissonance is to be told they are "overly emotional" or "dramatic" by their parents or caregivers who lied to them for the sake of control. This history may have also taken the form of gaslighting, prompting the codependent's inner dialogue to say things like:

- "I'm not doing enough."
- "I'm being too emotional."
- "I don't deserve this."
- "I'm being selfish."

External Triggers

These triggers might also be signs of danger you experienced previously. You may have learned to react to these signs in order to protect yourself from them. You may react negatively to such warnings and reminders, though it can be helpful in some cases. Because they might come from abusive or dysfunctional families, codependents may react strongly to situations that resemble experiences with their parents or caregivers.

Common reactions include:

- Feeling like you aren't doing enough.
- Needing to take responsibility for another person's problems.
- Not feeling worthy of someone's praise or attention.
- Feeling guilty for not being proactive with another's needs.

Many of these thoughts stem from situational experiences that are unique to the codependent and do not necessarily reflect the other person.

Practical Ways To Set Boundaries

Setting healthy boundaries is a must for codependents because it helps you accept personal accountability for your feelings. By doing so, you will cease to do the unhealthy behaviors while eliminating self-defeating beliefs that were keeping you trapped in the wrong mindset. In no particular order, here are the most effective techniques:

- **Get In the Practice of Saying "No" To Others**

You will find this mentioned many times over in this book because of its importance, but one of the most difficult tasks for a codependent to practice is saying "no" for themselves. Even if they know that what they are doing is not in their best interest, it doesn't feel good to turn down people who need their help.

Though you may be compelled to help, only you can set healthy limits if you learn how say "no" and have a voice separate from other people. The martyr syndrome is deeply engrained in codependents, and the result of saying "yes" too much is that the codependent loses themselves and their identity. If this is important to you, some suggestions of how you can withdraw from your over helping relationships: Evaluate what motivates you to say 'yes' a lot. There may be ways that you can alter your motivations so that you feel better about saying no.

Some alternatives that help to say 'no' are:

- "I feel uneasy or used when people ask for things from me"
- "I feel like I don't deserve to feel good."
- "I need to spend time or energy focusing on me. I want to value my own time and feelings. I want to know that I can say 'no' and still have people love me (in a healthy way)".

A negative thought pattern that many co-dependents hear over and over again in their heads is:

> "If I choose to stop helping others, they might become less interested in helping themselves".

This continuous inner dialogue can be hard to deal with-- you care about these people but they do not reciprocate in a healthy manner, and you keep giving more than you receive. The trick is to realize that they are not interested in your needs as much as they say they are. It may be true that they are self-absorbed, or it could be that they are so far down in their own self-destructive path that they don't even realize how much you do for them.

- **Be Aware And Accepting of Guilt**

Do you constantly feel guilty about everything, but do not know why? It is possible that you developed feelings of guilt because of a dysfunctional family. Refusing to help the person you love, can ultimately trigger guilt. Understand that these feelings come from old messages of not being good enough and are easy to let go of with some understanding.

Codependency is at its worst when you feel guilty for no apparent reason. The best way to deal with this is to accept your thoughts. Realizing that guilt is a natural byproduct of past experiences can be a relief. Take notice of your emotions and don't shy away from them. Stay open to these feelings and realize that they are what has been holding you back. Only then, can you find balance and move forward freely.

- **Accept That You Are Responsible For Your Own Feelings**

There is nothing wrong with providing support for a friend in need, but what if they keep treating you like a "fixer"? It's time to accept that you are responsible for how you feel about the situation and for your own happiness. This will mean you have to let things be, move on, and work on yourself. If that's more appealing than being bogged down in someone else's problems, then you need to remove yourself from the situation, and save your support for people who choose to really work on their issues.

To make this work, however, start by recognizing and examining your dependency on others. Doing this without blaming someone (including blaming yourself) can be difficult, but you need to recognize that those feelings might be coming from a codependent place. It's important to realize that you can't solve someone else's problems, so you need to ask if you are doing it to help yourself. While it's great that you want to make your partner happy, that is not your responsibility.

- **Identify Being Helpful vs. Being Codependent**

Giving to others is not a bad thing. However, not all help is great. Codependency can mean that the help you give others is controlling or unhealthy. So what is the difference between being helpful and being codependent?

Codependents are often driven by minimizing bad feelings and yet they often feel more sorry for themselves than those who contribute to their own problem. Being helpful, on the other hand, is one of the most important aspects of healthy relationships. It should always be about the other person and this does not have to cost you anything. The problem starts when this kindness becomes a responsibility that starts to drain your emotional well-being. If you're feeling guilty for not ringing your mother more often or having friends is a stress in itself, then you need to examine the level to which are you giving to others. Perhaps you give too much and need a more visible level of reciprocation.

There is a direct correlation between the amount of energy you give to others and the energy you'll get in return. You have the right to be selfish if you need to be. Knowing when you are truly being helpful to a loved one is critical in understanding how much "good will" your relationships have and how far you can go when reaching out.

Examine that relationship from the outside first. Be aware of the sacrifices you make, both in time and money. Ask yourself "Could this relationship survive without the extent to which I give?" Know that if the answer is no, you need to make a change in how much support you give.

Compassionate Boundary Setting Techniques

Setting boundaries in a compassionate way means addressing the underlying issues that come along with codependent behavior. The methods described below are a great example of how to do this, while maintaining a healthy relationship with the person in question. These include Radically Transparent Boundary Setting and techniques known as Shield and Sandbox.

Radically Transparent Boundary Setting

One method to understand and maintain healthy, enforceable boundaries is known as Radically Transparent Boundary Setting. This technique allows you to get your feelings across as you are feeling them in the moment. It welcomes others instead of driving them away. By acknowledging that setting boundaries can seem scary, you create a vulnerable position for the receiver. This creates an environment where they are more likely to engage in a conversation with you. You don't need to put on an act of being cold, perfect or confident in order to maintain a successful boundary.

The recipe for transparent boundaries is comprised of three parts:

1. Recognize that you are uncomfortable or afraid of setting a boundary.
2. Explain "why" the boundaries are needed.
3. Establish a clear boundary.

Radically Transparent Boundary Setting involves two key benefits. First, by doing so, you are acknowledging that initiating a difficult conversation can elicit negative feelings for both parties. This helps to show the recipient that you've considered how this boundary might make them feel. Secondly, when you clearly establish the "why" behind your boundary, you are reminding people that it is not an attempt to manipulate them, but to only protect yourself. You might want to emphasize your sincerity and openness, in order to maintain a strong bond.

Learning how to set healthy boundaries with loved ones—especially when codependent—is an important part of regaining control of your life. Listen to your thoughts and feelings when you create boundaries because it will be difficult to focus on everything at once. The decision making process can feel overwhelming from all angles, but allowing yourself to have a strong presence in your own life will help you realize that the reward is worth the work. This will take time and is very much like any other valuable relationship skill that must be practiced and learned over time. Forcing yourself to set boundaries with friends, family or colleagues will feel very unnatural at first. Remember that you're the one creating these boundaries for yourself and no one can do the work for you.

Expressing the "why" behind your boundary is important because it helps the other person to understand your perspective. When you ask for space or give an opinion about something, explain why it's so important. Explain that you're telling your friend what you need because you value the friendship and don't want to lose it. When you tell your supervisor that you need more time to focus only on work will you be more productive, your boss is more likely to agree with you. When people understand your side and give you room to talk, they're more likely to forgive and forget or give you space.

Realizing that setting a new boundary can be scary and that it might mean giving up the illusion of control over certain anxieties makes it a whole lot easier to move forward. Let go of the need to be perfect and realize that turning your life around starts with facing what might seem like scary confrontations. When you do it right, it's not that frightening. Being uncomfortable is part of the process. If you take control of your life and get ready to face those fears, then real change is in the works.

Be ready to explain why the boundaries are important to you when discussing with others. Letting people know how you're feeling and why boundaries matter to you will give you a sense of control. Being able to get boundaries in place will add a level of self-confidence you might not have felt in a long time.

Let's take a look at an example of this in action. Imagine for a moment, a close friend of yours has started treating you like a therapist, always wrapping you up in her family disputes and you feel as if the friendship is turning into a one-way street.

Using radically transparent boundary setting, you could respond in a few ways:

- "This is difficult, but I want to be honest with you. The reason I feel upset when we talk about your family problems all the time is because it makes me feel like I don't matter and like I'm just another listening ear."

- "I know we used to talk about your family and that I offered you advice and support. However, I cannot continue to be the primary person that you come to with your family issues and need more space."

- "I cannot be the only person you turn to when you need support. I want to help, but I know this relationship is important, so I wanted you to know that I'm not the person for this."

Start by setting small behaviors that are easy for the both of you; once they see how effective they can be, you can move on to more challenging situations and behaviors. Recognize those within your life whose attempts to control you have become a "trigger" for stress and anxiety. Of course, not all confrontations are created equal. Some take a bit more finesse than others. Pick and choose wisely and for each situation. Over time, with lots of practice, setting boundaries should become much easier to initiate and maintain.

Shield Technique

Some boundaries are like shields, providing us with an opportunity to defend ourselves against unwanted behavior. Shield Boundaries help protect us and help shield our time, feelings, belongings and things. They can be expressed by saying things like 'No, you can't talk to me like that,' or 'I'm sorry but I can't lend you money." They are generally short and to the point and typically say 'no.' They are a verbal form of self defense.

Sandbox Technique

Imagine a sandbox with things belonging to everyone. If you reach down, you can only pick up your own items. The boundaries of a sandbox are especially worrying for people-pleasers who are accustomed to carrying everyone's items out—not just their own. When we set boundaries and force ourselves to do less, we literally change our own patterns. We give up the old roles and relationships that we grew used to over time.

Healthy sandbox boundaries mean that the only things you take out of the sandbox are your own. Healthy boundaries help you distinguish what is yours and what belongs to others. The sandbox technique is a mental technique of being able to recognize when a problem is not your own.

Examples include:

- A co-worker is late on their deadlines and guilt you into helping them.
- A partner blames you for their drinking problem because you don't return their calls fast enough.
- A family member drags you into their custody battle with an ex.
- A neighbor places blame on you for not watching over their property while it was being vandalized.

Setting healthy boundaries means making life choices that do not focus on the needs you've learned to meet for others —it means focusing on your own needs. Healthy boundaries also mean that you honor each person's choices, and respect the choices they make for themselves, even when they are different from what you might think is best.

In Chapter 6, we are going to look at using the power of detachment to overcome one-sided relationships and develop your individuality.

Chapter 6. The Power of Detachment

When we are codependent, we don't have good boundaries and this means that we care about other people's needs without any regard to our own.

Detaching is an effective way to cope with this problem. It directly contradicts enabling because it lets you experience the consequences of your own decisions. Detaching can help you care for yourself and feel at peace by opening up the space necessary for emotional and physical recovery.

Codependents are people who like to care for others. Their desire to help is genuine but often ends up being useless. Caring about others can take away from caring for yourself. Detaching is a way to care for oneself, and avoid the guilt from taking responsibility for other people's poor choices.

For a codependent, the power of detachment is about releasing instead of clinging. If you cling, you are addicted to approval and attachment coming from others respectively; you're paralyzed. The reality of the situation becomes distorted. To detach is to see with clarity the patterns that trap you through illusions of reality and fantasy. If you're able to embrace detachment, you're not getting lost in a relationship. You can be addicted; you can even exploit; but if you practice detaching, then you become truly free. That is real empowerment. If you're attached, you're never going to be able to get out of it because you 're going to cling to the person, the cure.

Detaching is a loving action. It does not mean rejecting or abandoning others. Detaching from someone is the opposite of holding on tight or withholding love. To detach is to do less controlling, worrying, and giving all responsibility over to them.

The practice of detaching enables anyone to make independent decisions and allows space for the other person. It is much like setting appropriate boundaries. It gives you and your loved ones the freedom to make independent decisions. Detaching from others can be seen as untangling your life from their actions, so that your feelings and beliefs are not driven by something they do.

The Benefits of Detachment

You may have the impression that to detach means that you are being apathetic or selfish. But this is not true. We detach from others not because we are angry at them, but as a protective measure. Detachment is a way of caring about other people, even though they might not see it that way.

- **Detaching helps people learn and grow.**

Detaching is the process of setting boundaries with another person in a relationship and allowing them to make their own choices. It's a delicate situation, but an important one so that you can foster growth and independence while reducing your feelings of emotional dependency.

- **Detachment is the act of respecting a person's right to make their own choices.**

Letting go often means setting them free to take care of themselves, allowing them to have independence. Detaching is a skill that helps people be more balanced and stop reacting to every thing their loved one is doing. Detachment doesn't mean animosity or giving up on the relationship, but it does entail being emotionally self-sufficient. Codependence is driven by the fear that the person you love might not come back, so you hold on to them as a safety net. But this is what's keeping you from letting them be their own person.

The Importance of Detaching With Love

Detaching with love is a skill that helps people let go of codependent behavior. When we practice detaching, we stop overextending ourselves to others and let them solve their own problems. Detaching with love can help you if you're worried about your loved one, dissatisfied with their choices, or feel like every part of your life revolves around them.

Detachment with love means giving others the opportunity to improve and learn from their mistakes. Living detached ultimately means that one can let go and allow others to grow. It helps us stay less reactive and anxious, so we're less controlling. We also accept things as they are more easily in our lives. You need to detach when you care more about someone than they care for themselves.

It's difficult to change someone against their will. They may refuse to change and it can be frustrating and upsetting. It can be heartbreaking to watch a loved one self-destruct and it can be heartbreaking to keep trying to make them better. When you accept that you cannot change your loved one, detaching is the best thing to do.

You may think that detaching is mean or selfish. It's not. We detach to be healthy and live more authentically. Detachment is a way to take care of yourself, and in many cases in also the key to caring about others. It is a way to "stay on your own path" – that is, to focus on your own responsibilities, and not interfere with other peoples decisions.

The Processes of Detachment

Detaching is an ongoing process in relationships. It isn't a one-time event. It is an important component in overcoming codependency because it allows the individual to make decisions based solely on their own wants and desires instead of being swayed by another person's objections or requests. In the broad sense, there are two basic types: emotional and physical. They both differ in unique ways.

Emotional detachment only deals with thoughts and feelings within oneself, whereas physical detachment entails separating your self from the object of addiction or obsession, such as leaving someone or a situation.

Let's look at these two processes in more detail.

Emotional (or Psychological)

Emotional detachment is one way that codependents heal. They detach from other people's emotions and their own traumatic memories or experiences. It's a powerful technique for someone who needs an outlet to take his or her power back. Emotional detachment requires awareness of oneself and the world around you, as well as acceptance that you deserve to be happy. It involves practicing self-improvement and making personal changes. Furthermore, emotional detachment is refusing to wallow in the past or things you cannot control.

A detachment process can take weeks to months and isn't a skill that you can just turn on and off. It takes time and practice to build the inner strength necessary. Part of this process means not letting someone else's mood influence yours. It can sound like a way of cutting a person off, but this is not true. Detaching as a codependent allows you to be self-aware and understand your emotions.

Physical Detachment

What is physical detachment? For starters, it is not about turning your back on somebody in need. You cannot solve this problem from afar. It's about being less emotionally attached to someone while still caring about them. Physical detachment considers the bigger picture. It's about setting yourself free and staying true to who you are--even if that means you can't rescue someone else in this lifetime. Simply put, it's about loving people from a distance.

The physical detachment can be simply defined as the separation of the codependent from the person or thing they're depending on for false security, validation, and a sense of meaning. Physical detachment often continues even after resolving emotional attachment issues with another person.

Detachment Action Items

Separated by type, the following action items will help you take positive steps towards effective detachment.

Emotional/Psychological

- **Only focus on what's in your control.**

Understand what you can control and what you can't. Most codependents try to solve all their problems at once, and they always try to do too many things. Here's the solution: stop trying to be a superhero. The first thing you need to do is accept the fact that you can't control the other person. You can only admit your needs. Accept what will happen no matter what and try not to change them. Focus on things only you can control. Accept your partner for who they are. Don't see things as bad or good but just try to get some perspective on your situation.

- **Rather than reacting, take time to think before you respond.**

It's helpful to plan what you're going to say, rather than reacting on impulse. It's pretty normal to want to protect your loved one and take action the first time something is said, but it might not be necessary. Take time to think about what they're expressing. Is it really worth your energy? Do they just have a case of momentary insanity or are they asking for your help and you're not sure how to go about offering it?

- **Share your boundaries to let people know what you expect.**

The goal of setting emotional boundaries with another person is to take back your power in an emotionally abusive situation, and to become less affected by what others say or do. Before you can truly set strong boundaries, however, you must be willing to put yourself first.

Setting emotional boundaries is not about trying to hurt someone you care about or being mean, it's about loving yourself and being able to take care of what's best for you. You need to learn how to be assertive with your loved ones and tell them what you need in terms of respect, honesty and openness.

You also need to let them know what you won't tolerate. It can be very hard to do, especially with a significant other or spouse, but it is crucial. If you wait until things get out of control or totally unbearable before setting boundaries, you may feel guilty for hurting someone's feelings.

- **Take a moment and do something good for yourself.**

Notice what your needs are and try to satisfy them. Codependents are often super-involved in whatever they are doing with other people. They're willing to please others without considering their own needs.

The best time to start being good to yourself is now. One great activity is reading. Do something for your physical health. Go for a run. Dive into a healthy meal plan. Learn to get in the habit of taking those moments to do something that's a pleasure for you.

- **Allow people the opportunity to make their own decisions.**

Is it possible to love someone too much? No. Is it possible to take ownership of their decisions too much? Yes. The key to separating as a codependent is monitoring your own thoughts and feelings for judgment.
Let people make their own decisions. You shouldn't feel guilty about not being able to save them at every opportunity. People need to grow and you should let them.

Physical Detachment

- **Choose not to visit a dysfunctional friend or family member.**

If you have a friend or family member that drains you emotionally while giving little to nothing in return, then it is likely that your negative traits as a codependent are feeding their behavior.

The first thing that you need to do is redefine relationships. You should not get close to the person if the person is hurting you too much emotionally or physically. It may feel easier to show up again and again since you're trapped within your own guilt spiral. Choose not to visit and detach. You will heal in time, and realize your journey to health has nothing to do with theirs. You are still responsible for your life, and if that person will only tear you down with his or her abuse, choose not to follow their lead. Make an effort to detach from them as much as possible.

- **Take a time-out from an unproductive or hurtful argument.**

People who were raised in homes with addiction sometimes feel they need to take care of the people around them. Sometimes, you may be hyper vigilant when it comes to things such as finances or micromanaging a loved one's life to appease your own insecurities. This can easily cause conflict.

Fighting with the people you love is one of the hardest parts of being a codependent. You have all these feelings that want to be heard and seen and when you argue, it's all jumbled up. When things get hard, take a time out. A little break can do wonders for your emotional health and provide a great opening to resolve related issues peacefully.

Emotional arguments are never productive, and a person who is codependent may tend to get stuck in a cycle of negativity when faced with this. Emotional awareness gives the opportunity to detach from an argument and reduce pain caused by it - or end the argument and avoid a situation that is quickly becoming emotionally draining.

- **Avoid enabling or doing things others can do themselves.**

As a codependent person, you are dealing with two issues. You want to help the person you love and you feel like you can't stop doing this. Here is something that will help: avoid enabling them or doing things that they can do themselves (such as taking care of paying bills). Also, it is important to learn the difference between helpful and hurtful behavior. Codependents often do the opposite and therefore, they do not understand things from others' point of view.

How To Detach From An Unbalanced Relationship

One of the biggest things for codependents is to recognize when they are enabling someone in an unbalanced relationship. Emotionally, it might not make sense; if you are not receiving the care you deserve, then this puts your health and happiness at risk. Codependency is at its worst when someone in a relationship acts like an assistant. They are focused on what is being done for the person they care about. As discussed earlier, codependents in a relationship usually take on the "rescuing" role. They overextend themselves to try to help others with just about everything they're doing. Putting the needs of other people before their own is how they contribute to society and feel purpose in their lives.

If you are in a codependent and unbalanced relationship, you know how exhausting and frustrating it is. You probably feel that you need to do everything for the person who is still being uncooperative. And yet, instead of that person growing more loving, you find yourself in situations of increasing conflict.

Prevention is key if you don't want to fall into a codependent and unbalanced relationship with your partner. You have to be resilient, choose your battles and remember that it's not about you. But what do you do if you have already fallen into the pattern of a disproportionate relationship? The following methods will allow you to avoid enabling it any further:

- **Accept How You Are Feeling**

In order to stop enabling others, you'll need to start by acknowledging your own feelings. Sometimes this means facing your own behavior in harsh light and accepting any ways that you may have enabled a person even one time. You have the right to feel a wide assortment of different feelings. When you set boundaries, you might feel scared or heartbroken about what the other person will endure. It can be difficult when these unpleasant feelings occur. However, recognizing your feelings and letting them take their course is a necessary step in developing into a truly independent person.

- **Break Out of the Cycle of Denial**

If you want to change, you'll need to take an honest assessment of what your reality is. You don't have to keep living in the illusion that things are going well. The time has come to stop pretending that your actions are making it better. Codependency is an ongoing cycle of obsession, fear, and denial about an unbalanced relationship.

There are two main reasons why we stay in denial about something that's happening in our lives. One, because we want to avoid facing the painful reality or truth, or two, because we do not want someone else in our life to invalidate our projected reality.

Denial is a powerful thing. It can alter our thoughts, feelings, and senses by means of subtly manipulating our memory. The way we can move forward is to dig around in these denial pockets and find out where they're coming from. If you are in denial and you don't want to accept the uncomfortable truths about your codependent relationship, stop procrastinating. Step back and look at the facts. The biggest question you should ask is "How is this person making me feel?"

- **Remember to Focus on Yourself**

The problem with enabling others is that they might not be happy if you stop. It's important to focus on yourself and find what makes you happy. One of the ways to re-balance your relationship is to make sure you're spending enough time on your own self-care.

When you tend to focus on your needs and what you want, you will feel a sense of peace and calm. It's time you start building yourself up without relying on someone else. Strategies to focus on yourself include:

- Setting aside time for exercise.
- Engaging in meditation.
- Start a mood journal.
- Spend time in nature.
- Read a new book.

Taking a dedicated, proactive stance towards self-care takes discipline, but the rewards are worth it.

- **Always Detach With Love**

As mentioned earlier, detaching is the act of acknowledging that you do not always need to worry about what happens in someone else's life. You can love them, but they are not your responsibility. Giving unconditional love to people who don't respond in positive ways is not only bad for you, it can also enable them to stay stuck in loops of self-destruction.

Your feelings are not dependent on how other people feel so you can set boundaries without worrying. If they don't like your boundaries, separate your emotions from the situation. If they really care for you, they would have no problem changing themselves for you. Example statements include:

- "I feel upset when you act depressed."
- "I fear that you will fall into even more debt by not finding work."
- "I feel no joy supply you with alcohol, knowing that you cannot stop drinking."
- "I'm concerned that our supervisor will reprimand you for attempting to hand off your work to me."

By showing love, you are also decreasing the risk of dramatic conflict.

- **Accept Any Uncertainty That May Occur**

One of the hardest things for codependent people to do is to accept that they don't have control over a situation, because most codependents shy away from uncertainty. It may seem like an over-used cliché, but if you lean on others for acceptance, you know what you are getting.

What do you do when things are uncertain? You must accept it. If you are considering leaving a partner, it is okay to be fearful of what you life might look like or the uncertainty of a living situation. Once you truly and wholly accept that not everything is under your control, you will feel free. You'll be able to breathe deeply, knowing in the moment that it's all okay and it's going to work out - even if it doesn't look particularly pleasant in the moment.

Detachment is something you need to constantly work on. Understandably, detaching is a process that many codependents have difficulty with at first since it breaks a habit of sorts. However, you can do it when you work hard at it. You are much stronger than you think. Breaking free will enable you to detach from the chaos that your life is currently in. It will give you the peace and clarity you need. The good news is detaching is a process you can do at your own pace. Start where you are, practice and learn, and you will realize that detaching is not only practical, but also liberating.

In the next chapter, we are going to discuss how to put an end to an all too common habit among codependents—the habit of people pleasing.

Chapter 7. How To Stop Being A People Pleaser

Doing things for another's sake, might seem like a nice enough gesture. Surely, it's not bad to do nice things for people. However, people pleasing among codependents often end up being a negative experience as they ultimately sacrifice their own needs to gratify someone else.

People pleasers always try to keep others happy at their own expense, often at great length. It feels good at first but there's a problem with this behavior. Take a look around, how many people have you met that are easily "pleased?"

Codependency vs. People Pleasing

All codependents can be considered people-pleasers, but not all people-pleasers can be labeled as codependent. These two relational styles have some overlapping characteristics, like the desire to help and having trouble setting realistic boundaries. Codependency, however, is more extreme. To classify as codependent, the person on the receiving end of the connection is reliant on you for their own needs as well. You simply cannot function without each other.

People pleasers are driven by the need to get approval. You're probably a people pleaser if you have forgotten what your true colors were, what you want and need in life, and why you're on this planet. You might even find yourself trying to please people just because they're related to you or work with you.

We mistake selflessness as unconditional love. But what if a person cannot first love themselves? We're conditioned to think that if someone is a good person, they will be kind. But appearances can be deceiving. Kindness shows us what someone thinks, but not why they are doing it. Kindness can be one of the most difficult behaviors to fault. On the surface, kind actions may seem innocent, even virtuous. Society tells us that kindness is a virtue, and we should all commit to showing it. But when does giving go too far? When do we cross a line where selflessness becomes unhealthy?

In a world where the people-pleaser seems to reign supreme, it can seem difficult to break out of the mold we've been placed in. But with inner work and self-awareness, you can start making decisions that are more aligned with what you want in life and in business. Whether it's your boss, partner or friend, people-pleasing might just be a natural human behavior - and one that could ultimately leave you feeling more exhausted than fulfilled.

Giving ourselves up for others, prevents us from having relationships that are based on authenticity and closeness. Selflessness is often the sign of a virtuous person, but to provide too much attention to people can lead one down the path of not knowing what is in their best interests.

Origins

When you were a kid, didn't you want to make everybody happy? This included your parents, teachers, friends - the whole world. For some reason, that feeling of worthlessness and guilt ("What did I do wrong?") just never left us. Somehow we got it into our heads that trying to make every single person out there happy is what it means to be a successful human being. The problem is, no one can be all things to all people and by trying we are actually making ourselves miserable.

What motivates people to please others doesn't come due to their genes. Instead, we learn this as a way of maintaining connection and closeness with our parents. It turns out that many people pleasers begin their journey as "parent pleasers".

Parental inconsistency leads children to grow up feeling like they need to please others to maintain their connection. Perhaps due to their own personal illness, addiction, upbringing, or mental health, parents of people pleasers are often preoccupied with themselves. It becomes very difficult for the child when their parents are strong and loving, and then distant, absent, or worried. A child can't understand why their parents are showing affection one moment but being distant the next. These parents, in addition to grappling with their own personal issues, get tangled up with memories from the past and worry about the future.

When a parent has this conflicted style of relating to both themselves and the world, it is common for this trait to be passed onto their children. People-pleasing children soon learn that their parents are unreliable. But the child constantly turns to them, no matter what they do. At some level, they know that their happiness depends on how their parents are feeling about themselves.

Many parents are only focused on how to deal with their own problems and have no idea what their children might be going through. They might also misread their child's cues and emotions. In some instances, children take on the role of the caregiver to their parents and act more like an adult themselves. As a result, the parent struggles to stay emotionally available to their child. The child then interprets the situation as a signal to protect their parents so that they can remain connected.

So the child may become skilled at supporting their parents emotionally.
The child will be adjusting their moods and ensuring they are on their best behavior in an effort to make parents proud. They will be sacrificing what they want by allowing the desires of their parents come first and by not rocking the boat. And so they begin to develop their people-pleasing skills.

Children, however, often have a limit to what they can handle. When things get overwhelming, this usually results in unpredictable and surprising behavior. These children go back into hiding after the breakdown, hurting themselves with their own sense of shame. However, the cycle eventually repeats and becomes a never-ending circle that carries into adulthood.

Long Term Effects

If we define unhealthy pleasing as compliance without considering oneself, it is as though we're only living for others. When we do not share our unique perspective, it can harm both ourselves and those around us. If you think you have a people pleaser personality, remember that by caring for others more than yourself, you are making them responsible for your happiness. People pleasers seem frustrating and irrational to those who are self-reliant. When you give without considering yourself, it often backfires, and both the giver or receiver will also suffer. An over-giver can become exhausted and overwhelmed, making them unreliable. They end up over committing without thinking about how it will affect other people.

False kindness occurs when we give something without thought for how it may affect the other person. Though it seems like you're doing all this for others, you are pretty much just putting on an act. Pretending to enjoy doing things for another person isn't honest, and in the long run can create problems for you and your relationships. As a result, the following consequences can and will occur:

1. You Are Taken Advantage of By Others

Some people can recognize when a person is people-pleasing and take advantage of it. They may not know the name for the behavior, but know that you will agree to whatever they ask, and they keep asking. It is easy to feel pressured to always say 'yes'. However, this can have serious implications. You are more likely to be financially unstable if people ask you for money. Additionally, you would be more susceptible to being manipulated or abused mentally.

This behavior might manifest in other ways. For instance, you might be less likely to punish your child for skipping chores because you don't want to push them away. This will prevent your kids from learning life skills that they will need to be successful in the future.

2. You Become Angry And Resentful

If you do everything for others, they might appreciate what you've done, but others may not. They may not understand the sacrifices you're making. Hiding ulterior motives when being nice can eventually lead to anger and frustration. This often results in passive-behavior that just confuses people and upsets them without them knowing what's going on.

3. You Become Stressed

By putting others' desires before your own, you increase your chance of feeling stressed and overwhelmed. When you spend too much time pleasing other people, you may find yourself with less time for things you need to do. No matter how many basics you are trying to take care of, you may end up working long hours or not getting enough sleep, both of which will cause physical consequences.

4. Relationships Lack Fulfillment

Relationships depend on putting in effort and giving as well as taking. One person might do things for another, and be rewarded by being provided with the same treatment. However, you cannot hope to find fulfilling relationships by simply doing kind things for others.

5. Friends and Loved Ones Grow Irritated

A partner might notice that you agree with everyone, or apologize when you really should not. It's easy to let your relationship fall by the wayside while you take care of everyone else. Sometimes people-pleasing can backfire as you may take away their sense of independence.

Types of People Pleasers

There are many ways to please people. The following list broadly outlines the different types of behaviors.

- **Conflict Avoidant:** Going the extra mile to avoid conflict.
- **Emotional Caretaking:** When you really try to make the other person comfortable.
- **Compliance:** When you go with other people's values, interests, and opinions.
- **Active Pleasing:** You go along with the feelings and actions of others.

- **Merging:** Identifying with the preferences of your partner, friends or others, thinking that their choices are always the best even if they are incompatible with your own objectives.

Now that you have an overview of each type, perhaps you may have personally identified with one or two. This next section provides actionable steps to phase out of each role.

- **Conflict Avoidant:** Accept and prepare for conflicts. The closer to someone you are, the more likely there will be disagreements some of the time. When two different people are in a close relationship, it's natural that their needs and preferences will collide. Anger, frustration, hurt, and pain are all common reactions to being wronged. They are also common reactions to circumstances that go against our needs. We can be our own hero by acknowledging the feelings in ourselves and recognizing that they do not necessarily warrant leading to a fight. Conflict and fighting are not one in the same. The best way to think about conflict is to acknowledge it as the stage between negotiation and argument.

- **Emotional Caretaking:** You are not responsible if someone else is uncomfortable. If they are, it is their responsibility is to figure out why they're feeling this way. When we make assumptions about people, it's not fair and it can be problematic, even if those assumptions are coming from a good place. Removing the caretaking role is putting your faith in the other person's capability and decision-making skills.

- **Compliance:** We are all different. Your thoughts, feelings, and desires are what make you a unique person. Accepting yourself as a unique individual is a natural part of the process of becoming an adult. Sometimes, we are expected to be compliant, even if it's not in our regular behavior. The same way that we cannot always make others feel comfortable, it is also not our job to conform to what other people expect of us and play by their individual expectations. The people who do not treat you as a commodity will respect your individuality.

- **Active Pleasing:** From the outside, there isn't anything wrong with active pleasing. Intentionally thinking of what would make other people happy and then giving that to them is a lovely addition to relationships. The difference between altruism and people-pleasing is how much we are willing to compromise our own needs. It is often believed that it is virtuous to sacrifice oneself for others. The truth is, however, that active pleasing is the cause of frustration and eventual burnout.

- **Merging:** If we become so accustomed to merging with others, it can be really hard to know what it feels like not merging. We should remember that our own needs are just as important as anyone else's. It's important that we realize that no one is going to live our lives for us. We have the responsibility to do it ourselves.

The Pitfalls of Being Conflict Avoidant

When it comes to people pleasing, avoiding conflict can be a crutch that ultimately perpetuates dependence on others. Overextending yourself is a guaranteed way to feel taken advantage of. Here are a few ways in which pleasing others can end badly:

Giving with an agenda always backfires in the end.

When we only give in the hopes of getting something back, we are already forming a reluctant alliance. How can someone request a favor if they have no idea whether it would benefit or harm us? Here is a scenario:

Your friend asks to borrow your sewing kit for the weekend. You know you'll need it, because you promised to mend your son's soccer uniform, but you agree anyways. Since you don't want to let your friend down, you try to convince yourself that everything will work out. When your son asks about the tears in his uniform before the game, he is upset because you agreed to fix it. In this situation, the mother feels that it is better to avoid any conflict and, ultimately, disappoint her son.

A single "no" could have avoided this conflict, but pleasers tend to please whoever's around in the moment without thinking about what may come later. This scenario could be reversed by practicing self-care. Here is what it should have looked like:

You tell your friend that you need the kit to fix your son's uniform. You offer to lend your friend the kit next week after your son's game.

As simple as this seems, this presents the opportunity for a win-win situation.

In the long run, it is better to help someone with no expectation of something in return. People take advantage of those who are too generous. Regarding the same situation above, your friend wants to borrow your kit, but you remember she used it before and broke one of the settings. This same friend also borrowed gardening tools and hasn't returned them. You are beginning to resent the way she is always taking advantage of you.

In both these examples, there is a cost for everyone. In simple terms, these can be highlighted as the following:

- Repetitive conflicts
- Growing resentment
- Internal conflict and frustration

By allowing someone to take advantage of us, we are perpetuating their mistreatment of us and harming our own sense of self-worth.

Trying to please others without considering ourselves will strain your relationships.

We should be kind to ourselves, just as we are for others. We can be the most powerful voice for ourselves. In a relationship, it is important to say 'no' and be able to stand up for what you need. If we are unable to do these things, the relationship can soon become domineering and out of balance. If this pattern continues, then the pleaser will gradually distance themselves from the other person and pull away. Why does this happen?

Because when someone is alone, they can do what they want, without limits. Limitations don't exist when there is distance. In some relationships, the partner may step back because they believe that inequity in the relationship is wrong. Strong, life-giving relationships require openness and honesty. When the inequality in a relationship feels uncomfortable, it sometimes leads to distance. Relationships need to have appropriate understanding of each other, and this will lead to a better trust between both parties.

We need to care enough about another person to hear what they say, especially if we don't like it and the other person cares about our well being. Moreover, when we teach people to disregard others in interactions, not only are we disrespecting ourselves, but also the other person. The highest honor we can give someone is holding them to be their best.

Scarcity prevents the spread of love.

The more you give, the less you have. Overdoing leads to being unable to sustain yourself. Overspending means you will end up owing money. In order to be useful, you must first give to yourself so you can give to others without sacrificing your health. Yes, exertion is sometimes necessary for a worthwhile cause, however, rest periods are crucial to prevent burnout. Helping someone while resenting the act is a sign that we are tired or going against our values.

When we give because we are to afraid or too insecure to ask for what is needed, not only do we create indebtedness but we continue the cycle of feeling enslaved. When we do not set boundaries in relationships, dependency and selfishness can become destructive forces. Loved ones can also get hurt when you lie or re-tell them the partial truth to avoid arguments.

Adopting the Self-Directed Stance

Are you overly worried about pleasing others? It may be driven by underlying beliefs that are the cause of dysfunction. By adopting a self-directed stance, you will be less vulnerable to manipulation and can start setting limits with others. By changing your perception of conflict you may succeed in avoiding many unproductive disagreements.

- **Self-Directed Stance**

With a self-directed stance you can find peace in not caring about the approval or disapproval of others. This is where you can start to release excessive people pleasing in your life. It is important not to concern yourself too heavily with the positive or negative reaction of others. A self-directed stance should be cultivated.

Be yourself as best you can and even if the response from others isn't always positive, it is the right response for you. Many of us put pressure on ourselves to be without desires. If someone gives us a sideways glance or disapproves of something we are doing, we think "Oh no!" However, this is not a reflection of our self worth. Negative feedback from others is not always a true indicator of who we are, although it can be constructive at times. In the case of excessive people pleasing, a constant shift of focus towards the self is mandatory.

Being self-directed also doesn't mean that you have to be alone. Ask for help, and only take on what you feel confident doing. Don't stop from progressing because of other people's opinions. Being self-directed is about living for you. Do what you feel deep down inside that you can and want to do. Decide on your own values.

- **Self-Directed Individual**

An individual can easily maneuver between their needs and the needs of others, as they will always make choices that are in their own best interest. Playing the "leading role" in your own life means having the ability to make independent decisions. It is like trusting your gut feeling, and in that sense it seems that the goal here is to achieve more balance. Valuing your own independence allows you to become more comfortable with taking care of yourself. This in turn prevents you from having problems with feelings of self-doubt or a sense of being overwhelmed.

You need to learn to identify your own needs versus the needs of others. They could be legitimate needs or they might not. You can't solve the problems of everyone around you all the time. The important thing here is to look out for yourself, first and foremost. As you value your own needs further, you will find that you stop giving too much to others. As a self-directed individual, you'll find that your boundaries will be stronger and you won't let people step on you as often.

If you're obsessed with pleasing people, find the reason why you need to please them. Check for an underlying feeling of insecurity or a thought that you "need" someone's approval. Questions to ask yourself include:

- "Are you sure this person really needs what you do for them?"
- "How sure am I that they like the things I have done for them?"
- "Why do I think that this person will not appreciate or want to be around me if I'm not thoughtful towards them?"

Sit back and give yourself some time to be alone. You need to learn how to "be yourself" and to act on your own desires.

Practical Steps To Recovery

1. Before agreeing to something, think about why you're doing it.

Take into consideration the motivation behind each "yes" you give.

- Do you really want to do this?
- Are you willing to take on more responsibility?
- Are you agreeing for some other reason?
- Is it because you are afraid <u>not</u> to?
- Do you want to say 'yes' because they might do something for you without having to ask?
- Are you doing it because they made you feel guilty when you said 'no'?

Becoming more self-aware is the first step to changing your habits.

2. Set your boundaries for what you are willing to do.

Imagine the people in your life who ask too much from you without giving anything back. Reflect on your priorities and think about the people who may be taking advantage of you. Decide to what degree you want to commit to being available to them. Once you know what relationships are worth your time and energy, set those boundaries around the things you will or won't do.

When you know your boundaries, you can deny a request and still have control over your own life. If you're firm with yourself, it'll be easier to enforce limits when communicating with other people. Having boundaries can help you feel more in control of your life and focus on what matters the most.

3. Tell yourself it's okay to say 'no'.

Often the biggest problem when people are saying 'no' is that they think they're being selfish, uncaring or mean about it. Replying 'no' to what you don't want is essential to your interests. It's not only good for you, it's a human necessity.

Repeat the phrase: "I have the ability to say 'no' when I want."

4. Start saying no to the 'little things'.

Saying 'no' is just like any other muscle. The more you do it, the more powerful you become. And you'll find that the task will get easier in time. Think about what two things you could say 'no' to this week.

For instance, while at a clothing store, practice when the cashier asks "Do you want to open up a member rewards program?" or when a hotel clerk pushes you to upgrade a room when booking a business trip.

Fear often starts to surface when we first make changes. But soon we'll see that these fears rarely play out and that most feelings of discomfort pass after a few sessions. Just like starting a new workout, the first couple of days will be challenging. But after you've done it a couple of times, you will find that their reactions are never as bad as you thought. You will then experience a new level of freedom.

5. Keep your explanation brief.

To people pleasers, it often seems like they have a strong need to provide a lengthy explanation as to why they can't do something. However, a simple 'no' will suffice. You can politely reject a dinner invitation with, "Thanks for including me in the plans tonight. I really appreciate it, but unfortunately I have to decline". If a co-worker asks for your help, causing you to stay late, politely say, "I'm sorry, but I need to take my daughter to band practice."

6. You don't need to respond right away.

You might not be putting a lot of thought into your responses to requests, just giving a quick yes or no without really paying attention. Instead, take a moment and tell them that you will check your schedule and get back to them. You're also entitled to ask for more information. Start with questions like:

- How much time do you anticipate that this task will take?
- How many other volunteers will be helping out?

Remember that you have the power to negotiate the terms of your "yes" — don't feel forced into agreeing to something you're not completely happy with. You also have the power to make the request into a simpler task and possibly assume a smaller role.

7. Accept that saying 'no' will upset fewer people than you think.

People pleasers worry that when they say 'no', someone is going to be disappointed. This is not often true. When you stop people-pleasing, you realize that the person you said 'no' to probably wasn't as affected by your response as much as you thought they would be.

8. Do not offer help until it is asked for.

You are always willing to take on the things people don't want to do or offers ideas for when your friends mention any kind of problem. Next time, try to avoid volunteering your help until you've been asked for it. If your partner is talking with you about their day, don't tell them what you would do to be deal with it, just listen and show interest by asking questions in return. This is especially true if your partner goes off on a tirade about how terrible their boss is. Listen to them instead of offering advice. More than likely, what they want most is empathy and validation.

9. Put your self-care first.

When you are running low on emotional energy, you will be of no use to those around you. When you put your needs first, rather than ignoring them, it is not selfish. It is a healthy thing to do.

10. Show an act of kindness only when you mean it.

It's a positive trait to be kind to other people. But kindness doesn't come from wanting approval, and there is generally no motive other than helping another person. You should first consider your own intentions and how this act of helping someone else would make you feel. Is this going to make you happier? Will you feel bitter if a helpful act isn't reciprocated?

People pleasing is a common occurrence in our personal and professional lives. People want to get ahead so they will do whatever it takes to please other people, even if it doesn't work for them. A lot of people end up sacrificing themselves and reach a point of mental and physical burnout. People pleasing can be distracting, time-consuming and never-ending. It can feel good in the moment, but it also leaves us feeling constantly exhausted.

People-pleasing is a very common trait among codependents. Accepting that this behavior is an inevitable dead end is half the battle. Taking the time to make a change in how you respond to other's needs and demands is a critical component to the process of overcoming codependency. It's normal to want to please those around you and it's a universal desire. But in order to achieve success, we must have a clear understanding of ourselves first.

Chapter 8. Rediscover Yourself

It's tough to be a caregiver for so long and the pressure can make you forget about who you really are. Recovering from codependency is a personal process for every individual struggling with it. The one common denominator in any recovery process is self-forgiveness. Regardless of how long you have suffered and how low you have sunk, rediscovering who you are and what you find important in your life is the key to finding joy and fulfillment again. Obviously, recovering from codependency requires a lot of personal effort.

It starts with being honest about your problem, which probably is the hardest part about the process. You have to accept that you need help. Once you do that, the hard work of finding yourself can begin. This process starts with introspection. You will need to spend time alone reflecting on your past and looking at the ways you lived in the world through someone else's needs. Usually, people who are recovering from codependency end up dealing with other issues along the way. It is not uncommon to deal with depression or self-esteem problems during recovery. There is also a tendency for people with codependency to develop a negative relationship with themselves and lack a strong sense of identity.

Rediscovery is not always an easy process, but if you feel like you're drowning in your current life situation, now is the time to take firm steps towards change. Listen to your intuition and don't push it aside. It knows what you really need. When you're unable to find yourself anymore, it's probably because the person you became is done being part of your identity. There must be something worth saving deep inside your soul and fragmented memories. You are much more than obligation and expectations that you've conformed your life around. You cannot consistently feel satisfied, content or peaceful until you realize that your true self is waiting to come alive again.

Rediscovering yourself after spending years as a codependent means that you'll be thrown into the exact opposite of what you've been embracing your whole life and thinking in this way can make it seem insurmountable.

If you are the type of person who's afraid, overwhelmed or discouraged and wants to stop trying altogether then let me remind you that you're doing the right thing by ignoring these feelings, because they're nothing but a distraction from your true path.

Codependency recovery is not a linear process, but rather it reflects the rhythm of human growth and transformation. Understand that you're never too good to fail again. The key is that you approach every challenge with an attitude of humility, authenticity and willingness.

Self Awareness Exercises for the Codependent

The practice of self-awareness requires being fully cognizant of how we feel, who we care about, what drives us and what slows us down. It's all there in our psyches if we just take a moment to examine that inner world. And when it comes time to re-engage in relationships or tackle things that make us nervous, less anxiety awaits if we're clear-headed.

We become most aware when we learn to know ourselves, and this stillness of what we like -- what we don't like -- naturally keeps us in check. By doing any of the following self-awareness exercises, you can begin to get to know yourself. A few of the things you can try are:

Write down your thoughts, desires, and needs.

Pay attention to how you feel. Being aware of feelings will help because they'll directly reflect on that inner world -- an accurate map pointing toward emotional needs to be met. Paying attention to our inner world means living with, rather than running from, the distressing content that demands our full attention in the present. The most comforting course of action is to know when we are acting out a script and identifying where the pain is coming from. Finding the source often enables us to make sense of how we really feel and gain distance from codependent habits.

Start a daily journal and write down how you are feeling at both as you wake and before going to bed. Through this process you will be able to be more in touch with your emotions each day, outside of another person.

Be mindful about what you are feeling throughout the day.

Mindfulness is defined as being fully and wholly present and attentive in the current moment without judgment. The goal of mindfulness is to 'inhibit the impulse to act.' When you use mindfulness to be fully in the present, your knee-jerk reaction triggers of anger, fear, or frustration soften and begin to dissipate. Mindfulness helps you to change your relationship with yourself so that instead of relying on past (and negative) emotions to guide your actions, you bring all of these feelings into the present where they can end and you can experience the thrill of clarity and mindfulness. By practicing mindfulness, you will see how you often react out of habit and instead learn to respond differently when the same situation arises again. As a result, you will have more room to choose better, healthier actions free from codependent patterns.

Be mindful about what you are feeling throughout the day. Pay attention to what triggers or provokes both positive and negative emotions. Ask yourself the following:

- What am I feeling right now?
- What is currently going through my mind?
- Which thoughts are toxic and which ones pertain to my values?
- What is my most urgent need right now?

Become more aware of your body. Notice what you feel and any thoughts that coincide.

What does it really mean to be more aware of your body? It means that you can become more mindful of all the physical needs your body has. Take notice of all physical sensations and use them as clues for engaging your self -awareness in the present moment. Pay attention to your bodily sensations with curiosity. Rather than ruminating on these emotions and physical sensations, mindfulness can cultivate the ability to allow our own self to transcend and integrate biological stimuli with higher-order thoughts, emotions and cognition. This allows us to focus on the experience of just being.

Spend a few minutes being attentive to your body. Pay attention to your breathing, notice how your muscles feel, and listen to the sounds around you. Be aware of all of your sensations without judgment or analyzing. Think about how your emotions feel in that moment. Notice if you're feeling tense or calm. If you're feeling stressed, take a couple of deep breaths and focus on breaths extending to your stomach. If you're calm, does your body feel strong, focused and healthy? Or does it feel sluggish and weak?

Next, think about what your thoughts are. Are you engaged with a task at hand or lost in distraction and planning? Maybe you are ruminating about the past or worrying ahead into the future. Is doubt creeping in? Each physical sensation is a clue to what is happening in your body and mind. The more you put this into practice, the more you will start becoming aware of your authentic self.

When you feel down or uncomfortable, take a moment to figure out what you need. Then fulfill it.

Sometimes we are feeling so uncomfortable that we don't quite know what to do with it. We want something, but don't know what we need to fill that emptiness. This is especially true for the codependent who always answers the questions asked by their loved ones even if it's not what they really want. Many times codependents know how they're feeling, but they can't get in touch with their own emotions. They don't know how to identify what it is that's making them feel so uncomfortable, or why they feel this way.

The best solution for being in touch with your needs is to start making lists. Make a list of what is making you feel uncomfortable or distressed. For instance, you might write the following:

- I'm feeling the need for financial security and autonomy.
- I'm feeling fear that I am not skilled enough to do something that is unfamiliar or that my partner doesn't support my choices.

- I'm feeling anger that my needs are not acknowledged and validated.

Next, address your emotions or your feelings about the list itself. You might write, "I struggle to balance my fears of financial security with the expectations of my partner." Make sure your writing is clear and concise. Through identifying and attending to each item, whether in thought or action, you are perpetuating the autonomous function of your true self.

Create a list of what you 'want' to do and what you 'have' to do. Then compare the two.

There could be personal activities and routines you want to do, but there are times when you have chores that need completing such as cleaning or bill paying. It is nearly impossible to have the energy to utilize a system for personal improvement if you are tired from doing tasks that you have to do. Being aware of you wants and needs allows you to recognize any internal conflicts you are having. This in turn separates you from the codependent patterns of making others choices for them. Taking responsibility for your own life choices and commitments allows you to move forward by setting new goals that reflect those new desires.

Identify what prohibits you from doing what you want. Then take action to engage in the activity.

Codependents are more likely to have a difficult time doing things for themselves because they're always asking for help. If that's what's stopping you from doing activities you might enjoy, then it is time to celebrate your independence. No one is as special as you are, even if it can sometimes feel like no one notices. There is simply no reason to stop doing what you know is right for you. Part of taking care of yourself is knowing that you're important and deserve to have the things that you want. Knowing what you want is a major conflict for codependents and often the reason why most people with codependency stop and give in to what is expected of them.

It can be difficult for codependents to allow themselves to make their own plans. To overcome this, you simply have to face the fear of self-direction. After all, if you're having a really hard time making yourself happy, then the solution is to take action. You can start by making a schedule to do activities you might enjoy on your own. These can be quick, simple activities like going to a movie or taking a walk outdoors. The trick here is that you're going to make your schedule and stick with it. Start with the simplest things you can think of and write them in a calendar. The more often you do them, the less anxiety-inducing the decision making process will be.

- **Communicate authentically.**

Codependents are afraid to say what they feel and think because, in the past, their true feelings have been hurtful. They fear that others will reject the real them and that saying how they feel will cause a conflict or add stress to the relationship. It is difficult to trust that another person will react positively to your authentic self.

A codependent person can sometimes think that being unemotional is the best way to deal with other people. Sometimes, no matter how hard you try to find the right words and express yourself in a way that feels safe, you may hurt someone's feelings.

Pay attention to your feelings. If someone makes you upset, don't pretend that you are fine when you aren't. Make sure that you are out of harm's way but still express your feelings. If you expect people to react poorly because they have done so in the past-- yet they don't-- it can cause you shock and disbelief. "Wait, people don't get upset?" You might feel a sense of relief when this happens, but sometimes it can be disorienting to have the response you expected not manifest. Don't panic if this happens to you.

To begin being more real and authentic, focus on doing as much of the following as you can:

- Recognize your feelings and make note of them either in a journal or with friends if you feel comfortable.
- Start speaking to others with the feelings or opinions you would have previously kept close to your chest.
- Start your sentences with "I feel..." or "I think...," and continue with an honest, real opinion or feeling. As you make this a regular

practice when speaking to others, you'll find it becomes more natural.

Be assertive.

Assertive people feel good about themselves. When other people don't respect you, this will undoubtedly affect how you feel about yourself. You then become frustrated and are more likely to feel powerless. Yet, it's important to remind yourself that when you desire something and you're not getting it, it's up to you to change your approach. Assertiveness is an effective strategy for codependency recovery because it allows you to get what you want, as well as, respecting yourself for it. Good self-esteem will remind you that whether others approve of your actions or not, you always have the right to do what's best for your life. You are under no obligation to yield to pressure from someone else.

Being assertive means you are asking people to respect your boundaries without being patronizing. They should let you have your own opinion and accept your decisions or any other input that you give them. For example, if a conversation with someone is turning into an argument, explain that you care about them and that's why you disagree with their position; tell them you have to be honest. People with poor boundaries often accept criticism from others without considering whether negative input is coming their way because the person criticizing them cares about them.

Assertiveness doesn't mean you should stay quiet even when you are in the right, but rather stand up for yourself while conveying your position without making demands. Harping on others with words and arguments is a poor way to communicate; rather, you should do just the opposite: use as few words as possible to state your ideas. At the same time, never let others talk over you: make sure you get your point across before stepping back.

Have A Clear Focus For Your Life

Pay attention to your wants, not just answering the wishes of others. If you know what you want and focus on those things, you'll naturally start saying 'no' to others. This new clarity is helping you to declare your needs and wants. You are finally able to set a course and follow it. When you lack focus it's easy to go with what someone else wants.

What are the top 3 things in your life that mean the most to you right now? It could be your job, hobbies, family, or even downsizing. Take a few minutes every day to re-evaluate these priorities and write them down. Place the new list in a visible place like your bedside table so you are reminded of it each morning when you wake up. You can also make an additional copy of the same note for the fridge and your workplace.

These simple actions will help you remember your priorities every day and progress towards them.

Quick Tips

- Explore what self-care looks like for you. Has it meant taking a break mid-morning to enjoy your lunch at a nearby cafe, rather than staying at your desk and working through lunch? You may like to take a walk in the evening or go to the gym. Explore your options and make some decisions. Make small steps toward self-care by taking a break when tired and reading for fifteen minutes before bed. Get up and walk around for a few minutes. Try doing some stretches. Start out small.

- Imagine how much better your life would be if you were to refuse more often. Rehearse what you would say to a person when confronted with an invitation or request, and then visualize the result. This will help when it's time to set boundaries.

- Be open to saying 'no' more often. Start by noticing your response to requests. Then, when you're ready to reject a request, pause for a moment before responding. Take time to answer. Think about your response, even if you have to wait a few more seconds before acting impulsively. Make a time to look at your schedule and get back to them. Ask the person, "When do you need an answer?" This doesn't take much commitment and also gives you some space to reassess your decision.

- Distinguish when you are giving freely from your heart or when what you need to give up is unnecessary. Awareness is the first step in all of life's changes. Break habits by observing how it feels to give from a full cup. Then take note when you give up your wants, needs or desires to please others or to save someone from being disappointed. Your self-awareness will increase, which will allow you to make smarter decisions and avoid saying yes when it is not appropriate. You'll feel more fulfilled from giving to others and finding more joy in all aspects of your life. Bring your sense of self to the forefront by being more self-aware so that you may freely contribute, giving with a lot more enthusiasm.

Bonus: Ways To Get Rid of A Needy Mindset

Starting with a vicious cycle, codependents easily put themselves second and their needs last. Instead of meeting their inner need for love and approval, they meet the needs of other people to only have temporary closeness. This constant polarization stunts emotional growth and creates a perpetual "needy" mindset.

For a codependent, the prevalence of a needy mindset suggests a striving for affection, acknowledgement and acceptance. You care too much about what others think and it's beginning to impact your own mental health.
It can be hard to let go of a needy mindset, but here are five ways you can try to cut it out:

1. Accept that people can be happy with you one time and unhappy with you at another.

Sometimes, people's opinions can change. Seeking validation from others is unreliable and temporary, so embedding who you are based on that aspect of self is not only difficult but also completely inauthentic. We are simply too fickle as humans to be pleased by everyone. Sometimes people are happy with you, and other times they won't be. Their moods and preferences change, just like yours do. Needless to say, we are all a series of contradictions and are not perfect. Everyone is going down their own path, and some people are doing the best they can given their situation. People have different emotions and feelings that ebb back and forth throughout their lifetime. You need to be true to yourself and break your negative co-dependent bonds before they do further harm.

2. You can never please someone all the time.

Understand that the old saying is right, you will never please all of the people all of the time. You cannot be perfect, so someone is inevitably going to be disappointed. We have to learn how to accept people for who they are and their frame of mind at any given time. They may change their opinion even after a sober conversation, still that does not mean you should chase after them just to explain yourself.

As simple as it sounds, you can never please everyone all of the time. And you don't have to. To be truly happy, you need to realize that everyone is fighting their own little battles. See the good and the bad in people, without completely embracing either. If you look at everyone from a sense of realistic objectivity, you'll begin to separate from your co-dependence self.

3. Accept the negative reality of your current relationship.

Imagine the consequences of displeasing this person. If you realize that a person will probably react badly because of what you do, and also that your only motivation is to avoid this reaction, then ask yourself "Are the short-term benefits of this relationship worth as much to me as long-term losses?" If not, then you have created a conflict for yourself. There is no magical solution to this problem. You will find that there are costs and benefits for every action you take, and each one will have a long-term impact as well. You don't have to remain in that situation.

4. Understand that self-direction takes time to grow.

If you work all your effort into getting and keeping someone's love, then there is no time for your own personal development. Learn to listen to your intuition and develop your ability to make your own decisions. This takes both time and space, especially if you've been overly dependent.

5. Accept that simply because someone is happy with your current behavior does not mean that it suits you best.

It can be tempting to get the approval of others by giving into their needs, but it might be hurting you in the long-term. Simply because someone is happy with the current way you behave does not mean that it suits you. It can be tempting to get the approval of others by giving into their needs, but it might be hurting you in the long-term. I know that working hard for a loved one can give you great self-esteem.

However, in the end if you are miserable about it, it might not be worth it. Sometimes if it feels wrong deep down inside, you know you have to go your own way. Loving someone can at times be suffocating if they demand everything from you--including a fraction of your soul. They need to express their thankfulness for how far you've come in life by about how far to let you go for a while.

Becoming self-aware is a long process. You must start with committing to take responsibility for yourself and your actions, gaining the awareness about the way the codependency has been playing out in your life. This will help you to be self-disciplined, and having a more honest relationship with yourself. Help yourself to believe that you are worth it and that you are worthy of authentic inner love.

The next chapter will cover more practical exercises to improve self-awareness and ultimately separate yourself from codependent behavior.

Chapter 9. Self Assessment Exercises

This section covers exercises intended to demonstrate the extent of codependency in your everyday life. These exercises can be seen as checkpoints to assess the level at which you codependency manifests itself. There is no such thing as normal and abnormal when it comes to codependency. What matters most is that you learn how to recognize and accept your codependent tendencies in order to move forward.

Codependency Identification Quiz

Use the following quiz to see if you're codependent and want to learn how to focus on your own needs instead of the needs of others.

Read the following statements, then answer **true** or **false** for each.

1. I can easily put the needs of others ahead of my own. For me, helping others is a source of pride.

2. I find that I am focusing on the needs of others without even noticing.

3. I am in my best state of mind when I am giving advice or handling a crisis.

4. Sometimes, I have waited for others to take care of me to show their appreciation. But it never happens and I am getting frustrated.

5. Sometimes I become focused on one individual and only think about how to help them.

6. I usually turn down requests for assistance. I am uncomfortable when people focus their attention on me.

7. I think about other people when I am alone.

8. I am selfless and I spend a lot of time with my friends. People mostly like me because of how I can help them.

If you answered "true" to 4 or more of the statements, then you are most likely a codependent. Acknowledge your emotional responses but go lightly on self-judgment.

Next, pick one or two of the statements from above and write down when you observe these thoughts or behaviors in the coming week.

Statement 1:

_____

When and how this occurred:

_____

How did I feel?

_____

Statement 2:

_____

When and how this occurred:

_____

How did I feel?

_____

Codependency Origin Exercise

As mentioned earlier, family history plays a big role in the origin of codependency. If your childhood was filled with chaos or pain, you typically grow up lacking coping skills and assertiveness. This opens the door to caretaking because it feels safer than standing up for yourself and being alone.

One powerful step in identifying your codependency is to make a statement about how your family is dysfunctional. In order to heal, it may be helpful to face some of the things you have survived. Denying how you feel or forcing your feelings away will not help you get where you want to be.

1. Describe how your family is dysfunctional. This may include issues such as verbal or physical abuse, gaslighting, mental illness or poverty.

2. Are both parents dysfunctional?

3. Did your parents provide good care for you?

4. Did you start to see odd things as normal?

5. Did you feel shy and scared to have friends over?

Codependents usually learn to avoid their feelings in an attempt to stop everything from getting worse. The act of writing down or recording one's own history can often elicit feelings like anger, sadness, fear, and emotional pain.

You can even write a letter to your parent or guardian and tell them that you're writing it to let them know what it was like for you growing up in their home. However, you don't have to send it if you don't want to. This will free you up to revise and help you identify what you are feeling.

If you do send the letter, it's important to consider what your family will think before you share your experience with them.

Relationship Assessment Exercise

Spend some time thinking about the most important people in your life. This may include friends, a spouse, family members, colleagues, or a boss. Write these names down in a list. Consider how many people on your list are dysfunctional or may have untreated addictions. Are you the only one putting effort in the relationships?

Next, put your list away for 24 hours. Then identify the relationship that causes you the most stress and determine what boundaries you might set around this relationship. This will be difficult and cause stress, so do not try to do it in a single day, break up your thoughts over a week.

Practice telling this person about the boundary. It will probably be upsetting for him or her, but in the long run it will be beneficial for you both.

You need to be prepared to maintain the boundary that you set. Depending on the circumstance, you might say:

- I will not buy you any more alcohol.
- I will not call in sick on your behalf when you are hung over.
- I will not take care of your kids so you can go on frequent vacations.
- I will not loan you any more money, because you have yet to pay me back.

Every time you do this, you are taking another major step in your recovery.

Self Care Journaling Prompts

Writing in a journal is one way that you may express yourself and a way to identify some of your codependent behaviors and thoughts. Journaling is also therapeutic and can help you to become aware of patterns.

One of the primary goals in recovery work is building self-esteem without relying too heavily on external validation. These journal prompts will help you identify aspects of your recovery to work on.

Prompt 1. How can you focus more on yourself?

Make a plan for self-care activities you can do to make your life better. This can include planning your meals for the week, creating a new sleep schedule, or setting aside time for a hobby.

These small, often neglected aspects of life will help you feel more grounded. Give yourself permission to take some time for what you want to do and not always do what everyone else wants.

Prompt 2. What boundaries can you start setting?

Decide on one area of your life where you are willing to say 'no'. To start, identify the area where you feel overwhelmed and what boundaries you can set. For example:

- Can you remain quiet instead of volunteering for everyone?
- Can you scale back in any areas of your life?
- Is there a circumstance where you are exhausted from helping?

Prompt 3. How can you start to detach from unhealthy situations?

How can you detach from someone to find your own life again? Identify where you can slowly let go of someone who might be taking you for granted. You might also consider if you are helping someone who doesn't need it.

Prompt 4. How can you stop caring what others think about you?

When you start worrying about how other people feel, think about what you need to do to recover instead.

Write down different ways you can give yourself the acknowledgement that you deserve instead of waiting for others to credit you. Write down ways you can be kind to yourself if you've made a mistake.

Prompt 5. How can you make progress without trying to be perfect?

Embrace areas of imperfection that come with being human. Everyone has faults and quirks, which are endearing to those who love them. Where can embracing imperfection make your load lighter? Write down areas of your life where you can allow yourself to have flaws.

Prompt 6. Who can you ask for help or support?

Who in your life supports you? Consider seeking therapy if you think it would be helpful. Write down 1 to 3 key people who can provide you support when you need it.

Retelling Exercise

If in a troubled romantic relationship, most codependents enter a state of denial. They convince themselves that their partner's brutal actions, addictions or vices are no big deal. They even get jealous if the perpetrator seeks the attention of anyone else. They believe that their love and loyalty can change the other person for the better. Codependents tend to end up being involved with addicts, thrill seekers, or highly manipulating people. One of the effects of codependency is that it makes you perceive things differently.

To avoid these extreme pivots between imagination and reality, it's important to try to observe your relationship from an objective lens. Write down all the memories of your relationship. Start at the beginning. Pretend you are an impartial observer and only describe the facts.

Try to recall your memories with your partner. Write down different descriptions on multiple areas of their personality. This should show a full and dynamic image.

Read this story when you feel anxious or overwhelmed and need some perspective on relationships.

Self Care Meditations

Meditation can provide you with a sense of calm and objectivity. As I have discussed many times, keeping your mindfulness, self awareness and sense of choice as high as possible will help to keep you from getting sucked into codependent traps. It is a lot easier to push away intrusive thoughts when your mind feels like a sparkling clear pond. This is something that can be developed through practice, so don't give up and think, "I can't do this". The benefits of meditation are vast -- so try it as a different approach to combating intrusive thoughts

Meditation 1. Let Go of Approval

To do this meditation, lie or settle in a comfortable position and close your eyes. Breathe normally and focus on the sensations of the breathing. Pay attention to your breath. Notice how it moves in and out of your nose.

Notice what it feels like as the air leaves your body.

Repeat the word "breathe" while inhaling and exhaling.

Meditating without judgment means setting your thoughts aside and bringing your attention to your breath. Do this until the end of practice. Allow intrusive to thoughts enter and leave. Once you do this, you can work on managing your behaviors and breaking free from the cycle of codependency.

Meditation 2. Connect With Your Thoughts

For this meditation, try to focus on the natural gaps in between your breaths. Start by sitting in a comfortable position with your eyes closed. Take the time to notice what your body is doing, what you hear in the environment, and any thoughts or feelings that come up. Notice your bodily sensations, along with sounds from the outside world. Do not react. Breathe normally.

Mindfulness puts you in touch with your thoughts and feelings, which is the first step to discovering what you really want. This will take the focus off of what other people want, and place it back onto yourself.

When done correctly, the simple exercises in this section will allow you to claim your power back and put you on the path to recovery by reconditioning your codependent values and beliefs and incorporate a renewed sense of self awareness and self-respect.

Conclusion

Recovery from codependency can be very difficult. It is important not to feel guilty or ashamed of this struggle. You are a wonderful person, and you will heal. By reading this book, you are already on the path to healing. The process of recovery will be a long road but the good news is that there is hope. You can learn new skills and behaviors, which will set you free from your codependent life and the people who you enable. You can learn how to recognize enabler behavior and learn how to stop being an enabler. You can learn how to have both healthy relationships with others and be in a healthy relationship with yourself.

In this book, you have learned:

- How to let go of enabling behavior.
- Practical exercises to develop greater self care.
- Practical ways to set healthy boundaries.
- The power of detachment.
- How to stop being a people pleaser, once and for all.
- How to develop assertive communication styles.
- How to recognize and overcome the codependent narcissist trap.

In recovery, it is always best to reach out for help through a therapy group or a support group where you can find people who can relate to your problems. I also encourage you to consider a 12-step program for recovery. Many of these are available online as well as in your local area. Even if you have used a 12-step program before, it's a good idea to refresh your knowledge and your commitment to recovery. There are several different styles of 12 step programs and a few are linked in the resources section of this book.

Your journey to recovery starts today. You are not alone and there is hope for you.

Codependency doesn't have to be a life sentence. It is a learned behavior that can be unlearned. Take one step forward each day so you can discover what it is like to be your own best friend. You are worth it!

Resources

"Are You a People Pleaser or CoDependent?" *Locus Therapy Center*, 4 Mar. 2015, www.locustherapy.com/are-you-a-people-pleaser-or-codependent.

Bansal, Vinita. "Stop Being A People Pleaser: Don't Let Reward And Punishment Drive Your Behaviour." *TechTello*, 5 Mar. 2021, www.techtello.com/stop-being-a-people-pleaser.

Borresen, Kelsey. "How To Stop Being A People Pleaser And Learn To Say No." *HuffPost*, 9 Apr. 2021, www.huffpost.com/entry/how-to-stop-people-pleaser-say-no_l_606e2c65c5b6034a70844049.

Braime, Hannah. "The 4 Most Common Types of People-Pleasing (and How to Stop)." *Becoming Who You Are*, 21 Feb. 2021, www.becomingwhoyouare.net/the-4-most-common-types-of-people-pleasing-and-how-to-stop.

Cole, Terri. "Codependents + Narcissists – 4 Steps to Heal the Toxic Cycle with Boundaries." *Terri Cole*, 27 May 2019, www.terricole.com/codependents-narcissists.

Gaba LCSW, Sherry. "Escaping the Codependent-Narcissist Trap." Psychology Today, 6 Feb. 2019, www.psychologytoday.com/us/blog/toxic relationships/201902/escaping-the-codependent-narcissist-trap.

Garcy, Phd, Pamela D. "403 Forbidden." *Psychology Today*, 6 Oct. 2014, www.psychologytoday.com/us/blog/fearless-you/201410/needy-5-tips-stop-the-people-pleasing.

Gorkin, Mark. "Finally Letting Go of Relationship Codependency: Assertive 'I'-Message Beliefs vs. Blaming 'You'-Message Expectations -- Part II." *LinkedIn*, 28 Mar. 2019, www.linkedin.com/pulse/finally-letting-go-relationship-codependency-assertive-mark-gorkin.

Grey, Savannah. "How Assertive Are You?: Assertiveness Training for Codependents." *Esteemology*, 8 May 2017, esteemology.com/how-assertive-are-you-assertiveness-training-for-codependents.

Hughes-Hammer, C. "Depression and Codependency in Women." *PubMed*, 12 Dec. 1998, pubmed.ncbi.nlm.nih.gov/9868824.

Lancer, Darlene J. "6 Keys to Assertive Communication." *What Is Codependency?*, 19 July 2021, whatiscodependency.com/6-keys-to-assertive-communication.

Lancer, Darlene J. "Discover Your True Authentic Self." *What Is Codependency?*, 15 June 2020, whatiscodependency.com/your-true-authentic-self.

Lancer, Darlene J. "Are Empaths Codependent?" *What Is Codependency?*, 29 June 2021, whatiscodependency.com/are-empaths-codependent.

Lancer, Darlene J. "Acceptance Is the Beginning of Change." *What Is Codependency?*, 11 June 2021, whatiscodependency.com/accepting-acceptance-control.

Lancer, Darlene J. "Letting Go." *What Is Codependency?*, 19 July 2021, whatiscodependency.com/letting-go.

Lancer, Darlene. "Middle Stage of Codependency and Recovery." *Dummies*, 22 June 2021, www.dummies.com/health/mental-health/codependency/middle-stage-of-codependency-and-recovery.

Lancer, Darlene J. "Codependency Addiction: Stages of Disease and Recovery." *Psych Central*, 5 Dec. 2016, psychcentral.com/lib/codependency-addiction-stages-of-disease-and-recovery#4.

Lancer, Darlene J. "Early Stage of Codependency and Recovery." *Dummies*, 26 Mar. 2016, www.dummies.com/health/mental-health/codependency/early-stage-of-codependency-and-recovery.

Lebow, Hilary. "16 Codependent Traits That Go Beyond Being a People Pleaser." *Psych Central*, 22 July 2021, psychcentral.com/health/what-is-codependency-traits#codependency-vs-people-pleasing.

Lechnyr, Dave Lcsw. "Enabling Others: Encouraging Dysfunctional Behaviors." *TherapyDave*, 5 Mar. 2021, therapydave.com/codependency/enabling-others-encouraging-dysfunctional-behaviors.

Lindberg, Sara. "How to Let Go of Things from the Past." *Healthline*, 1 Sept. 2018, www.healthline.com/health/how-to-let-go.

Loverde, Mike. "What Is Codependent Personality Disorder?" *Family First Intervention*, 22 Dec. 2020, family-intervention.com/blog/what-is-codependent-personality-disorder.

Magee, Hailey. "How To Set Difficult Boundaries In A Compassionate Way." *Codependency Recovery Coaching*, 10 Jan. 2021, www.haileymagee.com/blog/2020/9/30/how-to-set-difficult-boundaries-in-a-compassionate-way.

Glass, Lori Jean. "Codependents & Boundaries: Why Do They Struggle?" *PIVOT*, 29 Nov. 2020, www.lovetopivot.com/what-cause-triggers-codependency-boundaries-recovery-coaching.

Martin, Sharon Lcsw. "Codependency and the Art of Detaching From Dysfunctional Family Members." *Psych Central*, 17 Apr. 2017, psychcentral.com/blog/imperfect/2017/04/codependency-and-the-art-of-detaching-from-dysfunctional-family-members.

Martin, Sharon. "How Codependents Can Stop Enabling and Controlling - Sharon Martin San Jose CA." *Live Well with Sharon Martin*, 27 May 2021, www.livewellwithsharonmartin.com/codependents-can-stop-enabling-and-controlling.

Martin, Sharon. "Codependents' Guide to Detaching with Love." *Live Well with Sharon Martin*, 28 Aug. 2021, www.livewellwithsharonmartin.com/detaching-with-love.

Rachelle. "9 Assertiveness Techniques to Use in Any Situation." *Info Counselling - Evidence Based Therapy Techniques*, Info Counselling, 15 Nov. 2017, www.infocounselling.com/assertiveness-techniques.

Raypole, Crystal. "How to Stop People-Pleasing (and Still Be Nice)." *Healthline*, 5 Dec. 2019, www.healthline.com/health/people-pleaser.

Raypole, Crystal. "What Are the Signs of Codependency?" *Psych Central*, 10 June 2021, psychcentral.com/lib/symptoms-signs-of-codependency.

Villines, Zawn. "Codependency and Narcissism May Have More in Common Than You Think." *GoodTherapy.Org Therapy Blog*, 7 Aug. 2018, www.goodtherapy.org/blog/codependency-narcissism-may-have-more-in-common-than-you-think-0807187.

Williams, Jennifer. "Why You Should Stop Being a People Pleaser." *Heartmanity's Blog*, blog.heartmanity.com/why-you-should-stop-being-a-people-pleaser. Accessed 29 Aug. 2021.

If you are interested in a 12 Step Program, please visit Codependents Anonymous at http://coda.org or American Addiction Centers at http://recovery.org.

33751607R00061